Affecting Change

Affecting Change
Social Workers in the Political Arena

Karen S. Haynes
University of Houston

James S. Mickelson
Oakland County Council for Children at Risk

Longman
New York & London

Executive Editor: David Estrin
Production Editor: Pamela Nelson
Production Supervisor: Judith Stern
Compositor: Intergraphic Technology, Inc.

Affecting Change

Longman Inc.
95 Church Street
White Plains, N.Y. 10601

Associated companies:
Longman Group Ltd., London
Longman Cheshire Pty., Melbourne
Longman Paul Pty., Auckland
Copp Clark Pitman, Toronto
Pitman Publishing Inc., Boston

Library of Congress Cataloging-in-Publication Data

Haynes, Karen S.
    Affecting change.

    Bibliography: p.
    Includes index.
        1. Social workers—United States—Political activity.
2. United States—Social policy.   I. Mickelson,
James S.   II. Title.
HV10.5.H34   322.4   85-19898
ISBN 0-582-29027-9 (pbk.)

86   87   88   89   9   8   7   6   5   4   3   2   1

*To those social workers
    who dare to enter the political arena
        and translate their ideas and ideals
            into actions
                for the greater good.*

Contents

Introduction

The current failure of the social work profession to assume a position of leadership in the movement toward social reform is inconsistent with its historical and philosophical background. The National Association of Social Workers' (NASW) Code of Ethics (1979) notes that social work's primary obligation is "the welfare of the individual or group served, which includes action to improve social conditions. Therefore, a commitment to this code is a commitment to social action."

The social work profession is in a unique position to contribute to our knowledge of the far-reaching effects of poor housing, inadequate education, and insufficient income. Yet, as a profession, social work has failed to speak out sufficiently about the inadequacies of the welfare system and other human service programs in both urban and rural communities throughout the United States. Today's social workers do not often seek nor are they asked to take a significant role in planning social programs or formulating social policy.

Although social work had its beginnings in direct practice, it has always focused on goals related to social justice and equity. Throughout the history of social work, interventive strategies consistently have been applied to relieve human suffering, right social wrongs, enhance functioning, and improve social conditions. It is clear that individuals, families, and small groups need help and attention at these levels. It is also evident that macrolevel strategies might effectively address these same areas for larger numbers of people and could simultaneously achieve permanent solutions to these problems.

It would be naive to suggest that individual social workers have not engaged in a variety of political activities. Certainly many in this century have taken an active part in social reform. However, throughout 60 years of social work education in the United States, content on politics, strategies for political intervention, and related skills have not consistently been included in the curriculum. Accreditation standards for graduate and undergraduate social work programs speak only in generalities about such political course content and coverage.

In fact, in a survey of 25 percent of all graduate and undergraduate bulletins for social work programs, only 6 of 122 different courses specifically focused on politics and political processes or included such content within currently offered policy courses (Haynes & Mickelson, 1985). Although political content may be included in policy courses and may not be explicitly noted in bulletin reviews, it is evident that political content is not of major substantive importance at either the graduate or undergraduate level.

Many have pointed out that the drive toward specialization and professionalization in social work is one factor responsible for the lack of interest in social action. Perhaps equally responsible is a lack of knowledge and training in the strategies and techniques fundamental to effective implementation of social reform. A commitment to social change without the means to achieve it is futile in any profession.

Social work received much of its early impetus a century ago from the social reformers of the day in settlement houses, neighborhood recreational and educational settings, and so on. But when the first training institutes for social work were established and university connections were formalized, content and practice in social work education took an individual casework approach, with the primary roles and tasks related to intervention at the individual level. During some periods of social reform, social workers were politically active, particularly during the postdepression era, when many social workers became involved in the creation of New Deal legislation. That decade introduced educational content related to group-work skills and community practice. However, the emphasis in practice and curriculum development swung back to individual reform during the 1940s and 1950s.

In the heyday of the civil rights movement and the War on Poverty of the 1960s, both the nation and the social work community were more focused on social reform. This resulted in the creation and implementation of major pieces of social legislation. Certainly the specialization of community organizations, if not originated during this era were at least enhanced, and many schools of social work consequently developed specialized community organization curricula. In reality, however, the relatedness of this macrospecialization to social work practice was minimal.

The 1970s shifted the profession and professional education toward increased emphasis on program and financial accountability, and graduate-level curricula dealing with the larger social work skills were directed toward management, budgeting, and program evaluation. In the mid-1970s, the National Association of Social Workers (NASW) developed both ELAN (Education Legislation Action Network) and PACE (Political Action for Candidate Endorsement), an important event that signaled the emerging awareness of the professional association between social workers and political activity. The purpose of both of these subdivisions of NASW was to affect legislative processes, with ELAN emphasizing lobbying and PACE working for the election of prohuman service candidates. Primary strategies for these two organizations were to educate social workers about legislation and candidates and to encourage social workers to support prohuman service issues and candidates and oppose antihuman service issues and candidates. Although both of these organizations have matured during the last decade, they are still in the embryonic stage of development because they have not yet become part of every state NASW chapter's organization. Social work education has entered the 1980s unprepared in the political arena despite the nationwide emergence of baccalaureate programs and the unparalleled growth of doctoral education in social work—developments that demand an emphasis on the differential use of social work manpower as well as a reconsideration of the core skills. Political activity and performance are still viewed as a matter of individual preference rather than as the intended outcome of social work education and training.

The 1980s have caught our profession short of social workers trained or even interested in political activity, either as a professional career choice or at least as an adjunct to clinical practice. With the turnaround in the 1980s from the expansion of federal monies for social programs to cutbacks, and as New Federalism returns decision making and, ultimately, funding of programs to the state level, it is becoming increasingly important for social workers to think about using interventive skills such as lobbying and campaigning for candidates. Although it seems evident that social workers are the logical professional group to defend and support human service programs, such support seldom has been forthcoming from either individual social workers or social work organizations. Even today some question whether social workers should be politically trained at all. Those who do support political training of social workers are left with the questions of how, by whom, where, and for what particular political positions.

In addition to the arguments already mentioned for including political content within the curriculum of social work schools and departments, there are distinct advantages to having politically knowledgeable and active alumnae. The most obvious advantage is the accumulated potential to create progressive social policy to deal with unmet needs, resolve social problems, or ameliorate unjust or inequitable conditions in society. The second is the ability to amass political strength for the promotion and for the protection of professional standards for human service personnel.

Last, because the majority of social work programs are publicly funded, a politically effective profession can be a positive influence on human service funding during the budget allocation process. Although this point may appear to be self-serving, one should remember that without sufficient funds to hire professional social workers, human services will be poorly delivered.

There are several ways in which social work education can interject political skills, experiences, and activities into the curriculum for students without shifting its emphasis. The first prescription for social work education at any level would be to include a political action course in the policy sequence:

rather than teaching the subject descriptively and historically, policy skills for practice would be taught. This in no way would run counter to the accreditation standards established by the Council for Social Work Education (CSWE) for bachelor of social work or masters of social work programs. In fact, the 1982 CSWE Curriculum Policy Statement notes that "the knowledge and skills students accumulate in these areas should prepare them to exert leadership and influence as legislative and social advocates, lobbyists, and expert advisors to policy makers and administrators. Social work students should also gain an understanding of political processes and learn to use them in ways that will further the achievement of social work goals and purposes (p. 5)."

Despite this statement of support and its attendant prescriptions for curriculum, one reason for the continued omission of political content in social work education is the absence of texts in this area. Because the goal of this book is to educate both social work students and social work professionals in methods of influencing social policy, it is our hope that the book will provide the impetus to add this missing component in the training of social workers. The emphasis on and inclusion of political content and skills in social work education must come from leaders within the field. This is essential not only to introduce this material into established programs, but also to ensure that future social workers have role models who view this career endeavor as one that is admirable and necessary.

Given the Reagan administration's massive cuts in domestic spending and the move toward more conservative, often antipoor and antiminority sentiment, social workers no longer can leave critical issues and decisions to nameless others. The rightful task and challenge of social work today should be to infiltrate the system in order to improve social conditions.

The rationale for this book was to discuss essential political skill areas that are not included in traditional texts on social policy. Our intent is not simply to describe political action skills and political processes, but also to pave the way for the integration of recognized political skills with traditional social work skills and thereby to create an effective and viable advocacy model.

Chapter 1 provides a brief history of social work political action so that readers will appreciate the origins of political advocacy. Chapter 2 illustrates the compatibility of social work values with political values. Chapter 3 examines several policy models that provide guidelines for examining policy and suggests interventive strategies appropriate to each model.

The way in which a practitioner's daily activities can culminate in significant input to the political process is discussed in Chapter 4. Chapter 5 describes several modalities that others have used to influence the political process, most recently the evolution of political action committees. The more traditional approach of lobbying is presented in Chapter 6. Chapter 7, "Monitoring the Bureaucracy," reviews the implementation of and subsequent adherence to legislative intent.

Chapter 8 provides an overview of campaigning, in order to enable social workers to assist in the election process. The final chapter presents the unique concept of affecting change from within the political system, as a politician. The glossary at the end of the book will help the beginning social worker to understand political jargon.

Suggested assignments of varying degrees of difficulty, complexity, and involvement are provided at the end of each chapter to assist in the development of political skills. Because this book may be used as a supplementary text, suggested readings are provided for further exploration of a given area.

REFERENCES

Council on Social Work Education. *Curriculum Policy Statement.* 1982.

Haynes, Karen S. and James S. Mickelson. "Politics in Social Policy: The Hidden Power Base." A paper presented at the Council on Social Work Education's Annual Program Meeting, March 1985.

National Association of Social Workers. *Code of Ethics.* Washington, D.C., 1979.

Acknowledgments

No book is solely the product of the authors. Therefore, we wish to acknowledge a variety of individuals who have contributed to this manuscript throughout its development. We list them in no particular order of importance. Each contribution was significant.

Given the stylistic differences of co-authors, we wish to extend our appreciation to Luanne Blackburn and Joanne Murphy for so successfully blending our styles. Additionally, we would like to thank Irv Rockwood for the final editorial touches.

No manuscript can be edited until it has been typed; therefore, we wish to thank Betty Phillips and Phillip Coffin for their secretarial support. Thanks to Shelley Baute, Janine Gauthier, and Colleen Pyle, student assistants at Indiana University, who searched for fugitive literature and analyzed data, and who provided general clerical support.

For assurance that the legislative terms contained in the glossary were inclusive, current, and generic, we turned to Patricia Currin, Jan Lindeman, Marion Wagner, Tom Watkins, and Toby Weismiller for review and comment.

We are particularly grateful to those social work politicians who took time from their busy schedules to provide us with insight and encouragement. We regret that they are too numerous to mention.

1
The Emergence of a Social Work Polity

Jeannette felt the cool fall winds of Montana on her face as she walked through the park, thinking about her past and about what the immediate future would bring. In just a few moments, the course of her professional life could alter dramatically.

She had known she was in the right profession when she received her degree in social work from a New York university. Yet, after practicing in various agencies, she had begun to develop mixed feelings about her work. She liked children and found meaning working with orphans and abused children, but more and more she felt empty and confused. Some difficult questions were on her mind: Why are children abandoned? Why are orphans treated poorly in institutions? Why are so many women beaten and left homeless by their husbands? Could one social worker really make a difference?

Jeannette understood that people have problems in the course of their lives, but it perplexed her that society didn't seem to care. Why did the government spend so much money on the military and so little on what she considered to be the country's greatest asset: the welfare of its children?

Jeannette knew she was good at her profession, but now she wasn't sure whether the new direction in which her career was heading would bring about help for the children. She was taking a hard road, yet she was convinced that it was necessary. She recently had spent many months traveling around the state discussing the problems that she encountered.

She knew that she could not continue working at the Children's Home Society. She found the job of locating homes for orphans intolerable. Seeing her clients traded like cattle or living under the deplorable conditions that existed in institutions, she became increasingly frustrated with the necessarily slow and singular efforts she made on behalf of these children. As an advocate for these defenseless and unloved children, it was impossible for her not to realize that many of the institutions' policies negated the positive changes she could make. She had come to know that the greatest possibility for reform was through influencing the laws that govern social institutions.

It seemed like only yesterday she had filed with the election commission to run for Congress, yet here she was today on her way to learn the election results. Competing with seven men had definitely been an uphill battle, but her background and knowledge of social problems had made a difference. If elected, her hard work in campaigning would pay off.

It took several days to tally all the votes, and in the end the Democrats swept the election—except for one instance: Jeannette won her congressional seat by only 7567 votes. On April 2, 1917, at the age of 36, Jeannette Rankin was installed as the first woman and the first social worker in the United States Congress (Lavassaur, 1984).

For Rankin, case advocacy for children led to a career in class and legislative advocacy. She lost her bid for reelection in 1919 because of her controversial vote opposing United States entry into World War I. Hers was the only opposing vote. The defeat did not stop her political activities, however, and she continued to work hard for women's suffrage and for reform of government policies toward children. She was reelected in 1941, only to vote again against American entry into another war, this time against Japan. She left her imprint on this country and its policies, on the peace movement, and on women's rights.

Jeannette Rankin portrays the transition and movement from individual to political reform today. Embodied in her, and in many of the early social workers of this period, is the simultaneous growth of social conscience, "scientific methodology," and macrolevel reform that logically emanate from individual problem solving. Her career exemplifies the fact that involvement in social action to meet human needs and improve social functioning is a logical outgrowth of social work practice. Clearly, today's social workers are the heirs of a powerful tradition of social action.

Although social action is not synonymous with political intervention, social action strategies, when used to intervene in the affairs of government, are political strategies. Furthermore, although social workers have been influential in the political arena, politics has not consistently been a central arena for social work practice. Consequently, a historic and ongoing dynamic tension exists between the two institutions.

During the decades of professional development following World War I the main body of social work may have turned away from its tradition of reform, but social workers never totally abandoned this tradition. In fact, the intensity of the debate over social reform changes with the general social climate. A lessening of disagreements among social workers on this issue not only will contribute to the unification of the profession, but could produce a multitude of interventions aimed at the formation and renovation of public policy.

No profession is in a better position to judge the impact of social policy than is social work. Although other professions direct their services toward specific problems, social work as a profession is involved with the overall impact on both the individual and the community of unemployment, inadequate health care, lack of education, poor housing, and insufficient income. Nonetheless, the social work profession has not systematically and consistently sought, nor has it been asked to take, a significant role in the planning of social programs or the formulation of social policy. Currently, there is increasing emphasis on professionalism within the field. Social workers should not be criticized for their efforts to attain professional standing, because acceptance of social work as a profession is basic to achieving the respect and authority necessary to effectively meet its obligations to those it serves. But the drive toward professionalism seems to have paralleled the profession's weakening concern with social reform.

> The coalescing and maturation of the trends in social work, in terms of the performance of a function rather than a cause, in emphasizing methods and techniques rather than goals, and in grasping for higher professional status . . . appear to be concomitants of the process of professionalization itself in the United States, but if this complex of trends continues, where are we headed? Three consequences are likely to follow. First, a continuing deemphasis on controversial social action which has broad social implications; second, a related lessening of attempts to influence social policy and the acceptance of the role of technician/implementor, and third, change in the ideology of social work that will lessen the gap its system of ideas and that of the dominant groups in society. (Bisno, 1969)

Indeed, social action has been deemphasized to the point that many question whether it really is the business of social work. In a 1972 study of 51 schools of social work, the majority of social work graduate students and educators did not consider social action or the initiation of social change to be a primary function of the profession (Carlton & Jung, 1972). A recent survey of undergraduate and graduate bulletins of schools of social work found there was minimal inclusion of course titles or descriptions that reflect political content or terminology (Haynes & Mickelson, 1985). Although these findings may reflect the professional schools' traditional bias toward the direct-service method of intervention, this bias is also found in many of our professional journals. A passionate but uninformed quest for relevance in activism is noted in one such journal as a factor responsible for the deprofessionalization of social work. Another journal asserts that "an activist spirit in social work downgrades professional practice."

In fact, the stress on specialization as well as some realistic legal restrictions (Hatch acts) has affected social work's participation in social action.

Today's social worker functions as a direct-service worker or as a manager, administrator, or planner, and there is little provision for operating at a level beyond or outside direct-service treatment and management. Only community organization work includes as a primary area of responsibility the taking of action to improve social conditions, and, unfortunately, training in this orientation is no longer provided in many social work programs.

The dominance of the direct-service orientation of social work methods is evident in professional schools of social work. Theories of human behavior are stressed to the relative neglect of theories of social change. Generally, professional schools do not furnish training in the strategies and techniques fundamental to effective implementation of social reform. The option of social action simply is not offered to most social work students, and a commitment to social change and reform without the means to achieve these ends is useless. Recent studies have suggested that holders of BSWs and MSWs ranked social policy and social legislation as among the least important areas of knowledge and skill (Biggerstaff & Kolevzon, 1980).

The failure of the social work profession to assume a position of leadership in the movement for social reform is inconsistent with its historical and philosophical background. The relatively nonactivist professional of the 1980s exists in stark contrast with turn-of-the-century reformers. A major characteristic of social workers of yesteryear were their efforts to direct the attention of the public toward social injustice (Meyer, 1970, p. 20), whereas a noted characteristic of social work since the 1970s is its failure to speak out about the inadequacies of welfare and other programs in urban communities as well as in the rest of the United States (Ginsberg, 1970, p. 19). Clearly, the profession's apparent reticence to address social problems that undermine the self-respect and morale of the individual is incongruent with its belief in the dignity and worth of human beings. How can a profession that regards the welfare of the individual or group as its primary obligation fail to speak out for social change?

It is our contention that professional social workers must oppose social injustice and, more important, intervene to right social wrongs. However, we repeat: It is insufficient and futile to promulgate moral imperatives without sensitizing professionals to these issues and providing them with techniques for successful intervention.

THE REFORM PERIOD

The Progressive Era (1895–1915) often is hailed as a proud moment in social work history. Early figures in social work have been lauded for their efforts on behalf of social action, and Jane Addams frequently is chosen as a model of the "involved" social worker. Caseworkers from charity organizations and settlement houses that existed in that era are heralded for having been in the vanguard of social reform. However, even though advocacy once occupied a prominent place in social work practice, and this function was highly visible early in the history of social casework, in examining the actions and interventive styles of this era in more detail, one notes that many social workers honored advocacy more with rhetoric than with practice.

Not only was the Progressive Era a prominent time for social work advocacy, these also were the years during which social work became established as an identifiable vocation. This era probably was the liveliest period of social reform and political advocacy in the history of the social work profession as well as in the history of the United States. Thus, it is not coincidental that the social work profession began with a focus on social reform. This was a direct result of the larger societal political climate at the time.

Social work during this period emerged from two separate interacting movements, both of English origin: The Charity Organization Society movement, which began in this country in the late 1870s and spread rapidly, so that by 1900, it had made its way into virtually every major American city and many smaller ones as well, and the Settlement movement, which took root in the United States in the 1880s and spread just as quickly.

By 1900, both of these movements were solidly established. Although their overall goals were essentially the same (protecting individual initiative and freedom), each movement's short-range goals and methods were quite different and frequently in conflict. The Charity Organization Society movement sought to reform on an individual level the character of those who were "losers" in society, whereas the Settlement movement worked to reform the social environment that made people "losers." The Charity Organization Society movement was not as oblivious to social reform as this oversimplification might suggest, but social reform was never its dominant theme, nor was the idea of reforming an individual's character totally absent in the Settlement movement.

Furthermore, a gap apparently existed between what was said by the Charity Organization Society's leadership and what was done by its staff and volunteers. The principles of scientific charity were never uniformly diffused or implemented. Although articles and agency records from this period contain some statements by social workers impatient to see the day when charitable relief with all its humiliations and harrowing uncertainties would be replaced by a fairer distribution of income and a complete system of social hygiene, education, and insurance, the Society's handbook seems insidiously pervaded by nineteenth-century Darwinism. It suggests, for example, that only two possible reasons could explain why a family with a father present would be in need of assistance: either the father is physically or mentally incapacitated, or he is handicapped by some defect of character or temperament (Sears, 1918; Lloyd, 1970).

Even during this period the social worker seemed to play more the role of facilitator or broker than of advocate. Although references to professionalization abounded in publications of the era, settlement workers were indifferent or even antagonistic to proposals for formalizing methods of helping. For this reason, their activities notwithstanding, settlement house workers did not significantly contribute to the development of social work methodology, but were more engaged in activities such as promoting factory legislation, better housing, adequate wages and working hours, arbitration of labor disputes, and providing free employment services. A passage from Jane Addams's *Twenty Years at Hull House* notes,

> We found ourselves spending many hours and efforts to secure support for deserted women, insurance for bewildered widows, damages for injured operators, furniture from the clutches of the installment store, constantly acting between the various institutions of the city and the people for whose benefits these institutions were erected. (Addams, 1940, p. 167)

Case-level advocacy was prevalent within the Settlement movement. Particularly in view of its espoused objective of improving living conditions, the Settlement movement epitomized the idea that a social agency should serve as an arena for the conversion of private troubles into public issues.

In summary, even during the Progressive Era reform period, case rather than class advocacy was the primary strategy of social workers. Furthermore, the translation of these skills into more formalized methodology did not materialize. Consequently, the decade of the 1920s left social work open to psychoanalytic theory and technique.

THE NEW DEAL AND BEYOND

With the New Deal era of the 1930s came another wave of political involvement by social workers. Although social action strategies were not necessarily well developed or formalized, the widespread recognition of social problems and the simultaneous identification of the public's responsibility for them provided broad opportunities for public policy intervention.

The massive social problems created by the Depression encouraged the development of a coalition of spokespersons for the poor, many of whom formerly had been apathetic or even hostile to the idea of public welfare. Consequently, during this era the social work profession became enmeshed in the national swing toward radicalism that was evident at the time in political parties.

By the 1930s, professional schools of social work provided a forum and a focus for critical thought about social service administration and the broader vistas of social welfare. However, their curricula still were somewhat disorganized and their primary emphasis still was on casework. The social work profession was not the leading faction in the nation's political–social reform movements, but a participant. Political activity was viewed by the profession as a short-term requirement for achieving its reform goals, but not as a legitimate social work method.

It was, however, during this period that Harry Hopkins, a social worker and political adviser, attained recognition as the controversial administrator of the first federal relief program in the history of the United States. His ascent from administrator of a temporary state emergency relief fund in New York (at the time the largest state relief fund ever created) to head of the Federal Emergency Relief Administration and then of the Works Progress Administration was unprecedented.

Although unfortunately he came to symbolize the lavish use of federal funds, Hopkins contended that these thousands of projects had not only fed the hungry, clothed the needy, and sheltered the homeless, but also had enriched the economy—ultimately affecting the lives of 15 million Americans. Because of his policies and programs devoted to mobilization of human labor power, he often has been hailed as the first national conservator of human resources in the United States.

THE WAR ON POVERTY

From the time of the New Deal through the 1950s, social work matured as a profession. During these years, the social casework method was refined and ego psychology became its dominant approach. United community charities and councils were developed to provide an organized method of meeting community needs. World War II and economic resurgence reemphasized individual dysfunctioning and, consequently, microlevel interventions. Social action was not a major emphasis during this period. Its absence set the stage for the subsequent renewal of professional interest in social action, which began to increase in the 1950s, as professional social workers saw that many of the issues that concerned them could not be dealt with through individual therapeutic methods. Social workers issued calls to undertake social action against the erosion of civil liberties under McCarthyism, against the arms race, and to support the developing fight for civil rights. Demonstration projects sponsored by the federal government and by foundations, such as the Grey Areas Project and Mobilization for Youth, provided a testing ground for new directions in community programs and new social work roles.

The mid-1950s were a landmark time for social work activity. The National Association of Social Workers was formed from the merger of several professional organizations, including the Association for the Study of Community Organization. The 1954 amendments to the Housing Act of 1949 required citizen participation in the formation of urban renewal plans, a requirement that set the stage for citizen participation clauses in other federal legislation. At the same time, a militant phase of the civil rights movement in the South introduced freedom rides, sit-ins, strikes, and protest marches.

Nonetheless, social action still was not emphasized in social work education, despite its use and partial legitimation in social work practice. Only a few practitioners and educators expected social action to become a major theme in social work education. As interest in social change spread, community organization became the focal area for students, practitioners, and educators oriented toward social change. Although community organization became a recognized methodological specialization built on a social action and class advocacy model, the general social worker's role was further removed from political involvement and intervention.

In the early- to mid-1950s less than 2 percent of all students enrolled in social work programs specialized in community organization. Community organization training was concerned with social welfare organization as a method of bringing about and maintaining adjustments between social welfare needs and social welfare resources. Preparation was primarily for practice in community welfare councils.

In 1955, Murray Ross presented community organization as a process in which community cooperation and collaboration could be built around problem solving. His formulation added new dimensions to community organization theory and practice. To the role of resource coordinator, popular in community welfare organizations, was added the enabler role. This practice method stressed helping communities to establish cooperation and reach goals by providing them with information and services in an objective manner (Ross, 1955).

Social Action Models   Attempts to respond to social changes gave rise during the 1950s to three models of social action in social work: "citizen social worker," "agent of social change," and "actionist."

The first model of social action, that of citizen social worker, is the oldest of the three. It calls for the professional social worker to use the information and knowledge gained through work with individuals and groups to inform the larger society of needed programs and policies. The citizen social worker confronts the problems of civil rights, international peace, equality of opportunity, expansion of social programs, automation and mechanization, suburbanization, and the need for preventive services as a concerned citizen, not as a professional obligation.

Many social workers came to embrace this model. Noting the professional social worker's responsibility for social action, Youngdahl (1966) states,

> First, we must have knowledge and fact, then we must derive our convictions based on these facts; this is followed by zeal to do something about them. It is not one or the other, that is, case work or social action; rather, it is taking advantage of every opportunity to be helpful to people as individuals, groups, or in society as a whole. (p. 132)

He goes on to say that social work, in trying to understand the individual, has made efforts to get at the causes of situations, and that our experience in dealing with numerous individuals has brought us to advocate certain social policies that will remove these causes and prevent the same thing from happening to others. This accounts for social work's broad interest in social legislation pertaining to housing, nutrition, recreation, and migrant workers, among others. However, according to this model, the primary reason social action is taken is because the social worker is an informed citizen.

The second model, agent of social change, developed in the late 1950s. Within this model, social action is defined as efforts toward purposeful change. The goal is to achieve desirable social goals utilizing well-developed and well-formulated theoretical systems as a guide to action.

This model developed new roles for the professional practitioner that emphasized active participation in an organization's political process. It suggested that social workers should directly be involved in political action and social policy formulation. These new roles were intended to produce change in institutional relations and policies via nondisruptive tactics.

Calls for a more aggressive professional stance in policy formulation were extended during this period. Many theorists suggested that social workers should enter the political arena and learn to deal more effectively with the community power structure.

In this model, the importance of working within agency or community structures is emphasized. The use of disruptive tactics, such as protests or strikes, is viewed as action that prevents the target system from continuing to operate as usual, and thus, as counterproductive.

The third social action model is that of the actionist. Actionists share the traditional social work concern for client groups but reject the detachment, insistence on societal sanction for the profession, and the belief that rational planning and cooperation are possible. They believe that social change, particularly for disaffiliated people or groups, can be achieved only by developing and using political, economic, or social pressure.

The actionist role is one of involvement with the client group the actionist seeks to help. The goal is to bring about desired changes based on what the client group identifies as its need. The selection of tactics or strategies is determined by whether they will be effective in achieving the desired goal.

The social actionist operates to a great extent on the basis of general principles, value considerations, and some operational instructions deduced from practice. The social actionist role is epitomized by the work in Chicago of Saul Alinsky and the People's Organization in the 1960s. The primary ideology of that organization was that "all groups are moved by self interest, the poor and the nonpoor alike; as soon as the poor and the victimized learn to see it that way, they'll be able to get power and control their destiny" (Alinsky, 1971, p. 41).

The actionist, although not opposed to using cooperation and collaboration as strategies, has more often been identified with attempts to develop power strategies. Actionists reject as confining the professional's identification with organizations and with social sanctions, and tend to view conflict and bargaining as the best method to bring about desired change.

What is important to actionists is the sanction of the group with which they are identified, rather than the social sanction of their profession. The actionist model stresses ideological identification of social work with society's victims: the poor, the mentally ill, the unfortunate. Central to this model is the need for social work to support the attempts of the disaffiliated to develop power and fulfill their needs.

Although the preceding three models provided direction and sanction for an array of social action strategies for social workers, the first and last models are not based on a social action orientation for the social work profession as a whole. Rather, they focus on the social worker as an informed and politically active private citizen and as a member of a temporary coalition.

With the national rediscovery of poverty in the late 1950s and the packaging of an array of federal programmatic responses to "cultural deprivation" and "pockets of poverty" growing out of the 1964 Economic Opportunity Act, social work once again had the methods and social sanction to engage in social reform. Community organizing, local community needs assessments, welfare rights advocacy groups, and "maximum citizen participation" clauses in federal legislation gave increased impetus to macro-level interventive techniques.

FEDERALISM

During the early 1970s, some of the reform ideologies and movements of the 1960s continued. Unfortunately, however, as the decade progressed and the War on Poverty programs became increasingly bureaucratized, social work practice and social work education turned its focus toward management and administrative theories and techniques, losing sight of advocacy and reform goals. As federal monies dwindled, competition for funds increased, and skills in grant writing, planning, and financial accountability took on more importance.

Despite some shifts away from social action, in a 1970–1971 report entitled "Social Work Education in a Period of Change," Arnulf Pins, executive director of the Council on Social Work Education, made the following comments:

Our nation, along with the rest of the world, is facing major social problems. Large segments of our population suffer from neglect, physical and mental illness, poverty, discrimination, and racism. Government leaders, citizen groups, and all professions must give immediate attention to the solution of these social and human problems. Social work has a unique role and opportunity. Consequently, social work education has a special responsibility and challenge, for it must prepare social work personnel with the commitment, knowledge, and skills needed: (1) to recognize and call attention to social needs, human injustices, and dysfunctional systems for service delivery; (2) to plan and bring about needed changes; and (3) to provide and administer social services in a more humane and effective way. (Pins, 1971)

Additionally, the leadership of the Council of Social Work Education testified in the early 1970s before the Senate Finance Committee, highlighting deficiencies in existing family assistance plans and seeking the inclusion in a proposed companion social services bill of funds for labor power development.

Furthermore, Daniel Thursz exhorted fellow social workers to consider one of a number of social action strategies. He debunked the common myths that have kept social workers from participating in many common social action strategies: the limits set by federal and state "Hatch acts," and false notions related to the profession's expertise, status, or dignity. In addition to the social action models of the previous decades, Thursz added civil disobedience, disruption, and "watchdogging" (Thursz, 1975).

The term *civil disobedience* refers to "any act or process of public defiance of a law or policy enforced by established governmental authorities, insofar as the action is premeditated, understood to be illegal or of contested legality, and carried out for limited public ends through carefully chosen and limited means" (Thursz, 1975). The important aspect of this definition is that civil disobedience is a method of social action to be used by persons unwilling to accept the rules of the system as a whole. Consequently, the social worker who participates in civil disobedience, regardless of his or her motive, must to be ready to pay the price imposed by society.

Most professional social workers do not condone violence. Disruption, however, is a social action technique that should not be confused with violence. Disruption may serve to call public attention to a cause and may serve as a prelude to new negotiations and advances in the relationship between an institution and the population it is expected to serve. The emergence of the National Welfare Rights Organization is a good illustration of this.

The watchdog role which Thursz describes, also called *monitoring,* is a social action strategy aimed at keeping institutions and their administrators faithful to a mission or policy objective. Administrators making complex determinations to establish criteria, determine eligibility, assess capability, evaluate past performance, or set a range of permissible experimentation have the power to advance or to thwart policy goals, to benefit or not to benefit the intended service recipient, and to realize or to subvert the democratic will.

According to Thursz, social workers should be watchdogs of administrative regulations to assure their consistent adherence to policy goals.

During the 1970s the social work practice and education changed in three important ways. First, with the increased emphasis on program and financial accountability, training in macro-level skills, particularly at the graduate level, was directed toward management, budgeting, and program evaluation. Second, a baccalaureate-level, professionally trained social work force emerged with the accreditation of BSW programs nationally. Third, doctoral education in social work experienced unparalleled growth.

These changes forced consideration of the differential use of social work labor power, as well as reconsideration of the core skills taught at all educational levels. BSW core skills included linking, advocating, and brokering; masters' level specializations were either clinically or managerially oriented, and doctoral education focused on research and education. Consequently, as the profession entered the 1980s, social workers continued to play a minimal role in the political arena and to view political activity as the result of individual, idiosyncratic preferences, rather than as a clearly stated objective of social work education and training.

However, some professional developments did occur during the 1970s that signaled the profession's reemerging awareness of political activities and processes. These included the National Association of Social Workers' (NASW) development of the Education Legislation Action Network (ELAN) and Political Action for Candidate Endorsement (PACE). These subdivisions of NASW were created to affect legislative processes. ELAN was to do this through lobbying and PACE through the election of prohuman service candidates.

The primary strategies of these two organizations were to educate social workers through the dissemination of information about both legislation and candidates, and to encourage social workers to support prohuman service issues and candidates and oppose antihuman service issues and candidates. These efforts slowly filtered down to the state level, with parallel functions being performed by autonomous state organizations. Although both of these organizations have matured during the last decade, in 1985 they are still in the embryonic stages of development. In fact, in many states neither of these organizations exist.

The 1980s have caught the profession short of social workers trained or even interested in some form of political activity, either as a professional career choice or at least as an adjunct activity that is to clinical practice (Wolk, 1981). The current shift in political thinking away from increasing federal monies and programs for social services, and the New Federalism's emphasis on returning decision making and funding of these services to the state level, make it all the more important for social workers to think about interventive skills such as lobbying and campaigning (Piven & Cloward, 1982).

CONCLUSION

The examination of almost 100 years of social work history suggests that over the years the profession has used a variety of political action strategies and activities. Playing roles that range from social worker as informed citizen to active lobbyist to federal or state administrator to politician, social workers have been engaged in political activity. Whether or not it is part of their formal role or training, political action has been part of social work history and will be part of its future.

It has been argued that any human service enterprise inevitably depends on community approval. Consequently, the choice facing social workers is whose approval to seek—that of the dominant establishment or of the exploited populations at risk?

Given the wave of massive domestic cuts in spending in the 1980s and the move toward conservative, antipoor, antiminority sentiment, social workers no longer can leave critical issues and decisions on social policy to nameless others. The rightful task and challenge of social work today should be to infiltrate the system in order to improve social conditions.

ASSIGNMENTS

1. Choose a period in United States history in which a major piece of social work legislation was passed. Identify the role of the profession or of individual social workers, or both, in its introduction or passage.
2. Choose one notable social work activist and trace his or her educational and experiential background.

SUGGESTED READINGS

Cohen, Wilbur. "What Every Social Worker Should Know about Political Action." *Social Work*, 11 (July 1966): pp. 3–11.

Davis, Allen F. "Settlement Workers in Politics, 1890–1914." In M. Mahaffey and J. W. Hanks (Eds.), *Practical Politics: Social Work and Political Responsibility.* Washington, DC: National Association of Social Workers, 1982, pp. 32–45.

Gilbert, Neil, and Harry Specht. "Advocacy and Professional Ethics." *Social Work*, 21 (July 1976): pp. 288–293.

REFERENCES

Addams, Jame. *Twenty Years at Hull House with Autobiographical Notes.* New York: Macmillan, 1940.

Alinsky, Saul. *Rules for Radicals.* New York: Random House, 1971.

Biggerstaff, Marilyn A., and Michael S. Kolevzon. "Differential Use of Social Work Knowledge Skills, and Techniques by MSW, BSW, and BA Level Practitioners." *Journal of Education for Social Work*, 16 (1980): 3, pp. 67–74.

Bisno, Herbert. "How Social Will Social Work Be?" In Paul E. Weinberger, *Perspectives on Social Welfare*. Toronto, Macmillan, 1969, pp. 304–318.

Carlton, T. O., and M. Jung. "Adjustment or Change: Attitudes among Social Workers." *Social Work*, 17 (1972): 6, pp. 64–71.

Ginsberg, Mitchell. "Changing Values in Social Work." In Katherine S. Kendall (Ed.), *Social Work Values in an Age of Discontent*. New York: Council on Social Work Education, 1970, pp. 13–34.

Haynes, Karen S., and James S. Mickelson. "Social Policy: The Hidden Power Base." Presentation at the Council of Social Work Education Annual Program Meeting, Washington, DC, 1985.

Lavassaur, Jean M. "Jeannette Rankin: Political Social Worker." Paper presented at Political Institute, Michigan State University, December 1984.

Lloyd, Gary. *Charities, Settlements, and Social Work: An Inquiry Into Philosophy and Method, 1890–1915*. New Orleans: Tulane University School of Social Work, 1970.

Meyer, Carol. *Social Work Practice–A Response to the Urban Crisis*. New York: The Free Press, 1970.

Pins, Arnulf. "Social Work Education in a Period of Charge." New York: Council on Social Work Education, 1971.

Piven, Frances Fox, and Richard A. Cloward. *The New Class Wars: Reagan's Attack on the Welfare State and Its Consequences*. New York: Pantheon, 1982

Ross, Murray. *Community Organization*. New York: Harper & Row, 1955.

Sears, Amelia. *The Charity Visitor: A Handbook for Beginners*. Chicago: Chicago School of Civics and Philanthropy, 1918.

Thursz, Daniel. "Social Action as a Professional Responsibility and Political Participation." In T. R. Pennock and John W. Chapman (Eds), *Participation in Politics*. New York: Leiber–Atherton, 1975, pp. 213–232.

Youngdahl, Benjamin E. *Social Action and Social Work*. New York: Association Press, 1966, p. 132.

Wolk, James. "Are Social Workers Politically Active?" *Social Work*, 26 (July 1981): pp. 284–288.

2
Social Work Values versus Politics

At the crossroads of competing values stands the social worker with a double historical task of urging movement toward the social good and rescuing those who have been lost or trampled on in the mass competitive rush toward personal affluence and social upgrading. The social worker ideally represents the social conscience of the community, prompting us toward action in keeping with our highest ideals; and the collectives of social workers should function in the same way in relation to their most earth bound members.

RUBY B. PERNELL, 1970

Policy—whether legislative, executive, or judicial in origin—may be defined as the operationalization or the compromise of a set of values, or both. *Values* are conceptions of what is desirable that influence the choice of action.

The social work profession, though a field resplendent with values, generally has avoided debates over social policy, ironically explaining its apolitical posture by pointing to its "values." The profession has denied that its refusal to politically intervene is, indeed, a political decision. Just as a clinician, after collecting data, may make a decision not to treat a client, so may a politically active social worker make a decision not to oppose a bill or not to support a candidate. If "no treatment" occurs at any level through inattention or neglect, the individual or societal consequences can be dramatic and damaging, regardless of whether this occurs on a clinical or political level.

The centrality of values to the origins and subsequent development of the social work profession preceded any concern with the development of theory or methodology. In fact, one of the most critical arguments in defense of professionalism in social work practice has been that the development of an independent set of norms, specialized helping skills, *and* humanitarian values enables social service work to remain autonomous, a power with the potential to offset narrow and repressive sectarian political interests.

Critics have argued that professionalism in social work has reactionary consequences. By supporting present societal values it may, unwittingly, strengthen society's repressive characteristics in the long run. The root of social work values may be a set of potentially conservative, system-conserving assumptions about individuals, society, and social change. Thus it is not that social work values are incompatible in general with politics and the political process, but that these values may be less than compatible with the profession's declared goal of public advocacy for societal/structural change.

Although social work values appear to be congruent with practice at the individual or small-group level (micro level), often they have been viewed as contradictory to the values and stances necessary at the larger, macro level of practice, particularly in administration. For example, social workers too often have acted as if budgets and fiscal considerations were not only inconsequential to their programs but also as if such considerations were inhumane. They seem to take pride in not understanding the issues. Social workers must learn that there is no incompatibility between caring, competence, and humanitarianism, on the one hand, and fiscal efficiency on the other.

This book is devoted to describing and analyzing the politics inherent in social work and the political functions served by social work as a consequence. In some chapters, the roles that social work does or should play in influencing political events are described, but, this chapter asserts that social work itself contains political theory and plays a political role. Social work practice, at both micro and macro levels, continuously acts either in support of or in opposition to the major institutions, policies, and values of our society. As such, social work is inherently part of the political process in the broadest sense, in that it is concerned with issues of either social conservation or social change.

Perhaps social work has not always explicitly recognized that any set of values, including those of "professionalization," entails a political position and, consequently, represents a position on the nature of the social order as a whole. "To say that social work is politics is to say, therefore, that social work in its every action represents political activity. Such activity is not limited to the usual arena called politics" (Galper, 1975).

With the exceptions highlighted in the preceding chapter, social workers either have overtly disagreed with this view of the inherently political nature of their work or they have been ignorant of it. The vast majority believe that social work is and should be apolitical. A recent national professional coalition (Project Human Serve) aimed at voter registration highlighted this stance. Social workers whose entire professional careers have been devoted to helping the less fortunate gain skills, education, and resources to enhance social functioning were indeed the opponents of social worker involvement in voter registration drives.

Indeed, the argument that the profession's values might be compromised has been used to impede the entrance of social workers into the political sphere. It is the intent of this chapter to describe the compatibility of social work values with political action and to suggest that these values often have been misinterpreted, but also to present arguments showing that in fact these values prescribe and mandate the intervention by social workers in the political arena.

SPECIALIZATION VERSUS SYSTEMIC SOLUTIONS

Among the important elements in any profession are the identification and development of areas of competence within which its members practice; the rights and obligations of the professional's relationship to these stated areas are thereby limited. The reason for this is twofold: to protect clients from a professional's involvement in areas that go beyond the professional's technical competence, and to protect the profession from general and undifferentiated demands made by its clients or consumers. This functional specificity is essential to professions in which great potential exists for intimacy between professionals and clients, because it structures working relationships such that clients view the process and the problem-solving methodology as specific to the problem at hand.

A problem with functional specificity that has long been apparent to the profession is that it creates a tendency—in fact demands—that the professional focus on and engage in only a piece of a client's life, and ignore other problems the person might have. Masters programs have created increasingly numerous, highly specialized areas of practice, derived from this idea of "professionalism." To the traditional specializations in physical health, mental health, and family and children have been added industrial, gerontological, substance abuse, and renal social work, to list just a few.

During the last decade, however, as the number of BSW programs has grown, a countervailing trend has emerged in the discipline, namely a growing concern with the integration and coordination of social services and with the development of generalist practitioners (BSWs) and case managers. Quite clearly, social work has been caught between two competing sets of values: functional specificity versus global or integrated solutions. Given that many clients have multiple problems, sometimes with a single cause, the artificial and narrow focus on one problem that is prompted by specialization may lead to an incomplete resolution. For example, a substance abuser who is also violent in domestic relations may be treated in a residential detoxification program, where the violence may be overlooked or assumed to be the effect rather than the cause of the substance abuse. Both of these problems also may be the effect of a third untreated problem, such as underemployment.

Inherent in the profession's emphasis on specialization is a more endemic problem: As social problems become the concern of a professional group, a problem-solving arena is created in which both problems and solutions are viewed as technical in nature, rather than as structural or political. Improving technology within social work practice inherently limits the way in which problems and solutions can be formulated. The resulting dilemma has been that the profession is unlikely to espouse changes on a broader level that could reorder or reprioritize society or societal values. That is to say, professional social work norms may well act as a set of blinders that induce social workers to prescribe easily implementable, technical solutions to problems that could be better addressed by other means. For instance, as child abuse came to be recognized as a societal problem by social workers technical solutions based on reporting and investigation systems were most frequently implemented, rather than political alternatives such as adding the "unemployed parent" option to state Aid to Families with Dependent Children (AFDC) eligibility regulations or increasing public support for day care. Although reporting and investigation systems certainly respond to the problem of unnecessary and critical delays in life-threatening circumstances, they are not solutions to the underlying causes of child abuse: poverty, adult isolation, and lack of adequate child care outside the home.

Another aspect of functional specificity that seems on the surface to discourage political involvement is the need to identify "turf." Social work increasingly has attempted (via licensing and classification efforts, for example) to define its role in relationship to other "helping professions" such as psychiatry, psychology, community nursing, recreational and occupational therapy, city and regional planning, and public administration. This has contributed to interprofessional rivalry rather than to building coalitions for the betterment of society. Perhaps even more debilitating than interprofessional rivalry is the existing intraprofessional rivalry between clinicians and administrators, between clinicians in mental health settings versus clinicians in health settings versus clinicians in school settings, and the like.

One can argue, therefore, that specialization, although necessary to professional definition and identification, may be antithetical to some forms of political action. If it is utilized as a clinical tool, however, rather than as an all-encomapssing value, it will not be a barrier to political activity.

SELF-DETERMINATION VERSUS COMPROMISE

Self-determination, frequently touted in the profession as the "king" of social work values, is certainly a cornerstone of social work practice. In its ideal form, self-determination gives the client the right and the responsibility to be involved in life choices and, of course, in treatment choices. This value derives from a belief system that imparts to all clients equal human worth and dignity, equal ability to enter into the decision process, and equal rights to determine for themselves the best choice of treatment.

Nonetheless, a number of inherent problems arise in the operationalization of this value. On the clinical level, it assumes that the social work practitioner has the knowledge and agency sanction to adequately and comprehensively present all treatment alternatives. In fact we know that quite often this is not possible. Particularly among specialists in social work practice, knowledge of treatment alternatives may be limited.

Unfortunately, social work education does not consistently and comprehensively provide information about community resources, eligibility requirements or accessibility issues. Thus, the array of alternatives suggested by the social worker may be artificially and even arbitrarily constrained by lack of knowledge, geographical limitations, or, as earlier noted, problem definition. Social workers also may find themselves in personal conflict with the professed policies of their agency. An obvious example would be a case in which a pregnant teenager is a client of an agency whose restrictions and policies prohibit the discussion of abortion as an alternative. Additionally, referral to an appropriate agency might be prohibited due to any one of a number of eligibility requirements, such as income, gender, age, residence, ability to provide payment for service, or language restrictions. Consequently, the array of alternatives provided to enable and support the value of self-determination often is restricted by the boundaries of a practitioner's knowledge as well as by agency practice (Keith-Lucas, 1963).

Equally important to the operationalization of this value in social work practice is its inherent assumption that all clients can actively engage in self-determination, when, in fact, many social work clients are unable to choose the best options because they have been unable to negotiate the larger system in an adequate manner. For example, a parent having a child with behavior problems might inappropriately be referred to an agency for counseling because the parent is unaware of the possibility of testing the child for learning disabilities.

Whether we view this failure to be knowledgeable about all treatment options as a personal or structural deficiency, it clearly diminishes the possibility of client self-determination. Whatever the cause—be it the client's age, gender, emotional or intellectual dysfunctioning—the result is an inability to choose rationally among alternatives that would be in the client's best interest. Young children, the aged, the emotionally disturbed, and the developmentally disabled are the most obvious examples of client groups for whom self-determination may be a meaningless notion. Social work practitioners therefore must see that it is well within their professional creed to assume an active responsibility for deciding the best treatment alternative for a particular client or client group. Many practitioners, however, even community organizers and administrators, feel that to make such decisions contradicts social work values by taking away rights from clients, and putting social workers in the position of being paternalistic and manipulative.

At the macro level, some social work administrators, researchers, and program evaluators have interpreted self-determination in operational terms that may speak against the long-term interests of clients and the profession. By committing themselves to an unbiased interpretation of data and the presentation of the full array of either funding or programmatic prescriptions, or both, they assume in others—funders, policy makers, and program designers—the same ability to be all-knowing and unbiased that practitioners have assumed in their clients. Unfortunately, administrative and evaluative decisions are not made often solely on the basis of the objective data presented; they are made on the basis of a set of values that may be unstated or unconscious, but nonetheless persuasive.

Social workers entering the political process tend to reveal their discomfort at being in the political arena. They want political candidates, elected officials, and administrative executives to have all available information rather than a biased and limited perspective, and the freedom to make informed and self-determined decisions. In a political process that has been built on competing political ideologies and values, this approach to macro-level intervention is naive, unrealistic, and too often supportive of the status quo. The problem is not the incompatibility of self-determination and political intervention but the perceived misfit. Although practitioners cannot implement self-determination in a pure fashion at either the micro or the macro level, at both levels this value can contribute in important and useful ways to promoting informed and humane decision making.

EMOTIONAL NEUTRALITY VERSUS CLIENT SELF-INTEREST

Another major premise of social work professionalism is objectivity or emotional neutrality. The social worker is strongly encouraged to become aware of and to control the degree of his or her emotional involvement with clients. The development and operationalization of this value has been said to represent the essence of the "professional self." Particularly in a profession such as social work, where the primary tool is the social workers themselves, emotional neutrality is required to differentiate professional exchanges from other kinds of person-to-person encounters. Without neutrality, the expertise of the social worker would not be publicly nor legitimately identifiable and sanctioned.

One potentially negative consequence of emotional neutrality is that it may induce social workers to deny or repress emotional experiences or emotional reactions. The isolation and suppression of emotions, however, may only serve to thwart justifiable anger and frustration at the social inequities that clearly are at the root of many client problems. Thus it may be possible for social workers to intervene with a low-income, multi-problem client and find short-term, ameliorating solutions, and at the same time to ignore the anger they feel toward the societal injustices that created the client's problems. If social workers were to become aware of and to express their feelings of anger at systemic and institutional barriers and inequities, a consensus might emerge that subsequently could lead to cooperative efforts at societal reform.

On a positive note, emotional neutrality may help the worker to continue practicing without experiencing despair or "burnout" in the face of enormous, overwhelming, and depressing social problems. At the macro level, many decision makers (both administrators and legislators) encourage a posture of neutrality because it supports the objective collection, analysis, and presentation by social workers of "hard data." Although collection and presentation of data are functions the professional must perform, restricting one's efforts to these functions may reduce one's effectiveness in being politically persuasive.

In providing legislative testimony, social workers too often have used indices of need, reported gaps in human services, and projected dysfunctions should a particular problem continue, to support their argument for improved service delivery to clients. Although these can be useful elements in a political strategy, what often has been missing is the descriptive, emotionally charged case illustration. Torn between a history of breast beating, at one extreme, and scientific argumentation, at the other, it may be that social work has swung too far in the direction of objectivity.

Social work lobbyists, for example, might prefer to present aggregate statistics about the probability that a proportion of the elderly in a midwestern state are unable to pay their heating bills, rather than to vividly describe the deaths of two old people due to exposure. The presentation of statistics not only might be less persuasive, but may mask real human suffering and pain caused by a particular inequity. Thus, emotional neutrality serves a useful function in a helping profession, but it should not be interpreted in a way that prevents the expression of justifiable and effective emotions such as anger at social unjustice.

IMPARTIALITY VERSUS PARTISAN POLITICS

Impartiality, as a professional norm, means serving clients without regard to race, religion, personal traits, gender, sexual preference, or political ideology. It suggests that professionals should stand above and apart from these differences and be available to provide service equally to all clients. For micro-level practice, it requires social workers to identify in themselves personal values and prejudices that may deter, influence, or mitigate against equal and impartial service to all clients. Impartiality is an essential professional value.

However, like the values previously mentioned, it has a potential bias, particularly when applied to macro-level interventions. Predicated on a limited definition of justice, impartiality can lead to unthinking support of the status quo—especially if equality and social justice are held to be synonymous with equality of opportunity. For example, although social workers supported the civil rights movement and the equal opportunity legislation of the 1960s, many of these measures assume that people start off equally. These laws and the programs they created attempt to guarantee equality of opportunity or of access without necessarily taking into account that people start life in unequal positions. Thus, measures to guarantee equal opportunity, however laudable, do not automatically guarantee equal outcomes for all.

In all societies, ours included, there is a scarcity of valued resources. As a political concept, impartiality, which has given rise to certain guarantees of equality of opportunity, may influence a more equitable distribution or redistribution of resources, by randomizing distribution across racial, gender, income, or geographic lines, but it does not alter the total available amount of a given resource.

For example, the Reagan administration has repeatedly argued that the federal government and federal budget should not be involved in any form of income redistribution; yet, in reality, income redistribution is precisely what budget and tax programs do. The issue, therefore, is the direction and extent of that redistribution. An impartial stance on income transfer programs may, in some administrations, be tantamount to support of redistribution of wealth to the upper class, which is what resulted from many of the tax changes in President Reagan's 1981 Economic Recovery Tax Act.

THE PROFESSIONAL CODE OF ETHICS

Any profession's code of ethics is both formal and informal. In either case, it is the articulation of a set of publicly professed values. The formal code is the written code to which professionals commit themselves on being admitted to practice. Within the social work profession, the formal code is exemplified by the NASW Code of Ethics. The co-existing informal, unwritten code carries the weight of the formal code's prescriptions.

Through its ethical code, the social work profession commits itself to certain values as a matter of public record, thereby ensuring the continued confidence of the community and formally obligating itself to client service. This kind of self-regulative code is characteristic of all professions and occupations, both technical and professional, but a professional code usually is more explicit, systematic, and to some extent more binding than an occupational code. As Figure 2.1 shows, the NASW Code of Ethic's major principles, as revised and adopted on July 1, 1980, not only specify a set of behaviors but also explicitly support the social work values previously discussed. Major Principle 6 states the social worker's responsibility for promoting the general welfare of society. A review and comparison of the first code adopted by the NASW and its revision (Gross, Rosa, & Steiner, 1980) notes the revision contains fewer articulations of this principle and the consequent prescriptions for social workers to engage in political advocacy. But despite the code's omission of substantial coverage of political responsibilities, it does not prohibit or negate such activities.

SUMMARY OF MAJOR PRINCIPLES

I. The Social Worker's Conduct and Comportment as a Social Worker
  A. Propriety. The social worker should maintain high standards of personal conduct in the capacity or identity as social worker.
  B. Competence and Professional Development. The social worker should strive to become and remain proficient in professional practice and the performance of professional functions.
  C. Service. The social worker should regard as primary the service obligation of the social work profession.
  D. Integrity. The social worker should act in accordance with the highest standards of professional integrity.
  E. Scholarship and Research. The social worker engaged in study and research should be guided by the conventions of scholarly inquiry.
II. The Social Worker's Ethical Responsibility to Clients
  F. Primacy of Clients' Interests. The social worker's primary responsibility is to clients.
  G. Rights and Prerogatives of Clients. The social worker should make every effort to foster maximum self-determination on the part of clients.
  H. Confidentiality and Privacy. The social worker should respect the privacy of clients and hold in confidence all information obtained in the course of professional service.
  I. Fees. When setting fees, the social worker should ensure that they are fair, reasonable, considerate, and commensurate with the service performed and with due regard for the clients' ability to pay.
III. The Social Worker's Ethical Responsibility to Colleagues
  J. Respect, Fairness, and Courtesy. The social worker should treat colleagues with respect, courtesy, fairness, and good faith.
  K. Dealing with Colleagues' Clients. The social worker has the responsibility to relate to the clients of colleagues with full professional consideration.
IV. The Social Worker's Ethical Responsibility to Employers and Employing Organizations

Figure 2.1 The NASW Code of Ethics Summary. (From National Association of Social Workers, *Code of Ethics*, Washington, D.C., 1979, pp. 1–2.)

L. Commitments to Employing Organizations. The social worker should adhere to commitments made to the employing organizations.

V. The Social Worker's Ethical Responsibility to the Social Work Profession

M. Maintaining the Integrity of the Profession. The social worker should uphold and advance the values, ethics, knowledge, and mission of the profession.

N. Community Service. The social worker should assist the profession in making social services available to the general public.

O. Development of Knowledge. The social worker should take responsibility for identifying, developing, and fully utilizing knowledge for professional practice.

VI. The Social Worker's Ethical Responsibility to Society

P. Promoting the General Welfare. The social worker should promote the general welfare of society.

Figure 2.1 (Continued)

CONCLUSION

Although the values discussed in this chapter are central values in social work, they by no means comprise an exhaustive list. Other important values include confidentiality, service, human worth, and dignity, but these values pose less conflict or confusion for professional social workers than do the ones we have discussed.

We have attempted to stress the importance and indeed the nobility of social work values. However, two important considerations remain: (1) an inability to operationalize these values into programmatic or legislative objectives, and (2) the leaning of many of these values toward preservation of the status quo rather than social change. It is difficult to imagine that these values are inimical to political strategies or ideologies. However, they are commonly misconstrued as being barriers to political intervention by social workers.

The intraprofessional debate about whether social workers should be actively engaged in political action committees and legislative lobbying—issues we will explore in greater depth in later chapters—in large part arises from this perceived conflict between political ideology and professional impartiality.

ASSIGNMENTS

1. Choose one of the social work values mentioned in this chapter. Illustrate first through a casework example, then through a political illustration,

the possible contradictions in utilizing this value as a means rather than as an end.

2. Interview three practicing social workers and ask them whether they think political activity should be a central part of a social worker's professional role. If so, exactly what activities should be undertaken? If not, why not?

SUGGESTED READINGS

Edelman, Murray. "The Political Language of the Helping Professions." *Politics and Society*, 4 (May 1974): pp. 295–310.

Gordon, William. "Knowledge and Value: Their Distinction and Relationship in Clarifying Social Work Practice." *Social Work*, 10 (1965): pp. 32–39.

Levy, Charles S. "Personal Versus Professional Values: The Practitioner's Dilemmas." *Clinical Social Work Journal*, 4 (Summer 1976): pp. 110–120.

REFERENCES

Code of Ethics. Washington D.C.: National Association of Social Workers, 1979.

Galper, Jeffrey. *The Politics of Social Services*. Englewood Cliffs, NJ: Prentice-Hall, 1975.

Gross, Gerald, M., Linda Rosa, and Joseph R. Steiner. "Educational Doctrines and Social Work Values: Match or Mismatch." *Journal of Education for Social Work*, 16 (Fall 1980): 3, pp. 21–28.

Keith-Lucas, Alan. "A Critique of the Principles of Self-Determination." *Social Work*, 8 (1963), pp. 66–71.

Pernell, Ruby. "Social Work Values on the New Frontier." In Katherine S. Kendall (ed.), *Social Work Values in an Age of Discontent*. New York: Council on Social Work Education, 1970, pp. 46–61.

3
Policy Models for Political Advocacy

One can view, affect, and evaluate the policy-making process in a number of ways. The choice of an appropriate political interventive action should be based on one's evaluation of the policy. Just as a clinician must examine the personal, situational, and environmental elements of a client's problem before reaching an appropriate diagnosis and intervention, the political strategist must holistically examine and then specifically focus in order to determine the appropriate intervention.

The similarity between determining a client's diagnosis and analyzing social policy can prove quite useful. In the same way that a client's presenting problem may initially be incomprehensible, social policy formation can appear complex and mysterious. To gain a clearer understanding of its various components, the client's problem or the social policy must be subdivided. This helps the clinician or the political strategist to identify the various components of the problem, determine the most important aspect thereof, and develop a plan of attack.

Within this clinical model of a generic problem-solving process that cuts across all levels of client intervention are all the steps and processes involved in political advocacy. For the clinician, the first step in the process is to get the client's view of the presenting problem. Intervention then requires a systematic collection of data to either substantiate the client's definition of the problem or to revise it. This data-gathering process, often called the *psychosocial history*, includes collecting information about the client's problems and significant relationships, his or her perceptions of these problems and relationships, and his or her interaction with the community and environment.

Likewise, the political advocate first must come to understand society's definition of the social problem. A needs assessment or social indicators analysis must then be conducted. This includes collecting data about the size and scope of the problem, identifying the primary population at risk, and outlining current policies and procedures that already influence or are influenced by current or new policy goals and administrative regulations.

After the collection of data, a clinician must assess or diagnose the client's problem. This step involves decisions about the scope of the intervention as well as whether it is change or maintenance that is required. The clinician must decide whether to provide treatment to the individual, to a dyad, or to a group.

On the political level, assessment involves identifying whether the appropriate intervention is administrative, legislative, or judicial, and whether it should take place at the policy formulation, implementation, or evaluation stage. The decisions involved in such an assessment move the social worker, whether clinician or political advocate, to develop the treatment plan or political strategy that seems most appropriate.

Ideally, at this stage each social worker should have an array of interventive models from which to choose. Clinicians may choose from a continuum of models ranging from the psychoanalytic to the behavioral to the client-centered approach. Likewise, political advocates may choose from among interventive approaches that view policy from various perspectives: institutional, rational, elite, group, or incremental. These perspectives will be explained later in this chapter.

Obviously, the next step in both the clinical and the political processes is execution of the treatment plan or political intervention, followed by an evaluation of the chosen treatment or intervention. This evaluation will result either in a termination of the process or in a repetition of certain steps in the process, so that a new or revised treatment plan or model for political intervention can be chosen.

As stated earlier, this chapter describes a number of methods by which one can review the presenting problem, develop an appropriate interventive plan, and evaluate that plan within a policy-making framework. It should be evident from our presentation, analysis, and illustrations that the choice of an appropriate political strategy should be preceded by an analysis and definition of the problem, a selection of the appropriate policy model, and a design for policy evaluation. The prescriptions for advocacy, presented in this chapter supports this book—to teach political intervention skills.

MODELS DEFINED

It would be extremely difficult, if not impossible, to develop strategies for political intervention without a clear understanding of the available models from which the political advocate may choose. Just as the caseworker chooses a model because of its appropriateness to the client's problem, taking into consideration pragmatic constraints of time, money, or situation, so too the political advocate chooses from a model that focuses on what appears to be the most critical area for intervention, taking into consideration whatever practical realities the environment, budgets, or political climate might dictate.

A model is a representation of some aspect of the real world designed to yield insight into or to focus attention on a specific segment of it. Models deliberately oversimplify reality in order to permit understanding and to direct intervention. Therefore, models quite necessarily treat some variables as crucial and ignore others, in order to appropriately focus attention on a limited and specific array of determinants (Dye, 1981). For example, the psychoanalytic model deliberately excludes such explanatory variables as environmental and interactional data, but it is nonetheless useful in clinical treatment.

Similarly, policy models should simplify and clarify thinking about social policy and political intervention by identifying the important aspects of a policy and the targets of political intervention and by predicting policy consequences. A useful model should clearly identify the important aspects of a policy, using concepts that are testable and have commonly shared meanings. It should be able to explain phenomena, not simply describe them.

Institutional Model   Much political activity clearly occurs within governmental institutions, such as Congress, state legislatures, courts, and political parties. Technically speaking, a policy does not become a "public" policy until it has been enacted, implemented, and enforced by some governmental institution. The institutional model focuses on policy as the output of these institutions.

This approach may focus on a structural examination of governmental institutions, but to be most useful it must go beyond that to include examination of the linkage between structural arrangements and policy content. This model focuses on questions such as these: Are the policies of federal social agencies more responsive to social problems than are the policies of state or local social agencies? How does the division of responsibilities among mental health services affect the content of social welfare policy? Both of these questions require not only a description of structural institutional relationships, but also a projection of the outcome of the policy as the result of those relationships. When utilizing this model, one effectively focuses on structural arrangements that seem to affect policy outcomes.

For example, most states deliver general assistance to the poor through state- or county-level agencies. However, Indiana still maintains a township trustee system as the vehicle to deliver this service. Consequently, 1008 separately administered and autonomously directed poor-relief services exist within the state, without any state-mandated standardized procedures for determining eligibility or benefit levels. Not surprisingly, this results in extensive variation across townships and unequal and inequitable service to clients. For several years now, political advocates have sought legislation that would assign responsibility for general assistance to a county-level agency— a structural solution to the problem.

In general, interventive strategies based on the institutional model will focus either on altering organizational structures or on choosing an organizational level or division within which to introduce structural change.

Process Model   The process model views policy as a political activity. In contrast to the institutional model, the process model focuses on how decisions are made. According to this view, it is neither the structure of the organization nor the content of the policy that is of primary interest, but rather the activities entailed in the policy-making process. This approach may appear to be of limited use in the analysis of policy, but it is extremely useful to the strategist trying to influence policy.

If, for example, you studied the way in which bills are processed by legislative committees, you probably would obtain information that would prove useful in future lobbying on behalf of measures you support. To do so, you would need to determine the types of data and evidence the committee was willing to consider. Did they assign greater weight to written testimony, expert opinion, or empirical data? Did they regard verbal testimony, client or consumer opinion, and experience as valid evidence? Knowledge of the specific types of data considered and the weight given to each might prove to be crucial information to an intervenor.

For instance, as multiple agencies vie for a limited number of dollars, they often have to make presentations to the funding source to support their budget requests. Understanding the decision-making process is essential for successful competition. One Area Agency on Aging, for instance, obtained partial funding when it presented a well-prepared budget and position statement at the legislative budget hearings. This testimony was fully supported by empirical evidence on the number of elderly in the area, average incomes, age distribution, and marital and health status. This information documented the need for funding of homemaker, congregate-meals, and medical-pre-screening services. On the other hand, the local rehabilitation center had not only prepared verbal testimony accompanied by empirically supported evidence of need and documentation of the number of clients served, but the staff also brought to the hearing several paraplegic clients to give personal testimony for the need of extended services. The dramatic emotional appeal of this latter strategy led to full funding of the request from the budget committee.

Additional information useful in this analysis might be information about committee composition, such as the background of committee members and their current positions within the legislature; and knowledge of specific pressures on the committee or on individual committee members, such as the total committee agenda and popular constituent opinions. The strategies likely to be suggested via this model include interventions in the committee processes, and attempts to influence their outcome most probably through lobbying.

Group Theory Model Individuals with shared interests commonly group together to strengthen support for their demands. When these demands are made on a governmental institution, they become part of policy analysis. Sometimes direct-service agencies with similar goals band together (or cooperate) to strengthen their political clout. The group theory model is characterized by its central focus in the analysis on interaction between political groups.

Often the group is viewed as a vehicle for transmitting ideas and demands from individuals to the government. In this model, politics is seen as a struggle among groups to influence policy making. Changes in the relative power of one group vis-a-vis another are expected to determine changes in public policy. The relative influence of a group is related to its size, the resources at its command, its leadership, and its access to decision makers.

In the group model, policy formulation and implementation are the result of negotiations between competing groups. If we were to apply this model in a study of policy-making processes concerning reproductive rights, for example, we would focus attention on the positions taken and tactics used by significant interest groups. Thus, we might examine "right to life" groups and Planned Parenthood coalitions by studying their membership, tactics, and strategies. We also would be interested in collecting data on the resources available to these groups (such as time, money, or membership), in order to determine why one group may be more successful than another within a given legislative session or have more appeal to a certain constituency.

In the group theory model, the management of intergroup conflict via the establishment of rules (such as ceiling on campaign contributions) that facilitate intergroup compromise, and the enforcement of such compromises is seen as the primary function of the political system. Compromise, conflict resolution, or the gaining of victory by one interest group usually are seen as processes that foster the national interest, and the results are said to constitute public opinion. This last assumption, however, is valid only if all groups have or are ensured equal access to power and resources.

Using this model, a policy advocate might try to influence decision making through access to the decision makers or through the control of scarce resources. Intervention strategies could include building coalitions with the controllers of resources or the formation of political action committees. Thus, if a reproductive rights advocacy group was having limited success in legislative lobbying because of its small numbers, active opposition, or public denial of the issue, a possible strategy would be to form a coalition of agencies representing multiple issues. This would provide the advantage of collective persuasive power and might mask the more sensitive or controversial issue.

Elite Theory Model Elite theory views public policy as largely de-termined by the preferences and values of a governing elite. Elitists hold that the general population is, in general, apathetic and seldom attempts to make policy or express values. Further, public policy is seen as reflecting the views of the elite, who generally belong to the higher socioeconomic strata and are not representative of the general public.

Consequently, change is slow and the status quo will be preserved unless and until societal shifts alter the elite's self-interest. This is not to imply that elites will always work against the general public's best interest, but rather that it is this group who defines the public interest.

Because this model assumes that the general population is either ignorant or apathetic, and views institutions such as political parties as being primarily symbolic in nature, its focus is on elite behavior and preferences. It also tends to assume a consensus among the elite regarding fundamental norms and values.

Using this model, it is possible to argue that even major pieces of social legislation have been introduced or supported by the elite, not by the "masses." This model is helpful in examining for instance, the relative ease with which Medicare and Medicaid legislation was enacted in the mid-sixties, compared to the uphill, and as yet unsuccessful, battle over nationalized health insurance. According to this model, the difference is explained by the fact that Medicare and Medicaid affect the upper-income elite only mini-mally, whereas nationalized health insurance could jeopardize consumer choice and increase health care costs for all, including the elite.

Utilizing this approach, an appropriate strategy would be to convince the elite group of the value of the desired policy change and to work with them to achieve it, possibly by getting elected to public office and becoming "one of them." You would need to advocate not only why the policy is good, fair, or just, but, more importantly, that it will be in the elite's self-interest.

Rational Model The rational model could also be defined as an effi-ciency model. That is, a policy is most rational when it is most efficient in achieving maximum benefits. Consequently, what characterizes a rational policy is that the ratio of benefits to costs is more positive and higher than for alternative policies.

The model assumes that costs and benefits of a particular policy can be known, that all policy alternatives are available, that all policy consequences are measurable, and that cost–benefit ratios can be calculated. Further, this model assumes that social values can be defined and weighed.

One of the barriers to an informed, rational choice among policy alterna-tives is that to eliminate a policy already in place may be extremely costly. Another is that long-term benefits, however predictable, must be weighed against current budget considerations. If, for example, we examine the Women, Infants and Children's (WIC) program, we see that despite clear evidence that every short-term dollar invested in the program saves three dollars in health care costs in the long run, funding for WIC continues to decrease and support for this program continues to be limited. The only "rational" explanation for this is that current economic decisions outweigh decisions favoring more efficient, long-range policy outcomes.

The rational model allows us to calculate and evaluates costs and benefits not only on the basis of the group of clients, consumers, or populace directly affected, but also on a larger societal level. Obviously the definition of beneficiaries will determine the cost-versus-benefits ratio of a particular policy.

Using this model, one would compile information and data to be utilized for purposes of persuasion. Arguments showing that the advocated policy change is more efficient—that it enlarges the potential beneficiary group and the long-term positive outcomes of a policy—are strategies for winning policy changes that will increase benefits.

Incremental Model The incremental model views current public policy as largely a continuation of past policies, marked only by incremental changes. One of the best-known proponents of this model, Charles Lindblom, suggests that decision makers normally do not review the entire range of existing and proposed policies, rank order their preferences among all alternatives, and then make informed choice. Constraints of time, money, intelligence, and politics prevent such a comprehensive, rational approach (Lindblom, 1959).

This model is conservative in that it utilizes existing policies as baselines for determining the range of possible policy change. One of the advantages of this approach is that it is less costly in terms of both time spent reviewing and projecting alternatives, and the costs already invested in existing policies. Consequently, it is a more expedient political model.

Using this model, you would focus on new or potential policies only in terms of their relationship to existing ones. An example is the addition of the unemployed parent (UP) clause to the Aid to Families with Dependent Children legislation. This clause would enable two unemployed parents to receive AFDC benefits without having to separate. Rather than totally reconceptualizing and dissolving the present AFDC policy in order to enact a guaranteed annual income, some states simply added this UP provision to their AFDC program. Following the incremental approach, one would look for policies not dramatically different from existing ones.

A PROACTIVE APPROACH TO POLICY DEVELOPMENT

The problem-solving strategies utilized in any field are only as good as the theories or models available. Social work does not, however, have one model that is adequate to encompass processes and outcome as well as the etiology of the social problems to be addressed. Most of the previously mentioned policy models can be characterized as follows:

1. Reactive to crisis and remedial in orientation
2. Residual in response, reflecting a reluctance to intervene
3. Based on existing capabilities of special interest groups to influence decisions amenable to them
4. Supportive of stability and therefore of existing patterns in distribution of resources
5. Only marginally responsive to inequities in society (Humberger, 1977).

These criticisms imply a need for a systemic or holistic approach to the examination of public policy. Humberger suggests a political–economic approach to examining the dynamics and interrelationships among political, economic, and administrative variables that impact the human service field. He suggests that such an approach is useful for both macro- and micro-analysis.

Humberger's approach is not significantly different from a systems approach, which, when applied to politics, includes examination of the political system, the external environment bringing pressure upon that system, and the output of the political system—public policy. This approach allows, even demands, that variables be examined in a holistic fashion. It suggests the examination of variables not only as they interact within a particular sector, be it administrative, legislative, or executive, but also as they interact across sectors. For example, a state's decision to mainstream special education children would be viewed as a policy decision affecting the special education sector as well as the social welfare and education sectors, as affecting not only special education students, but normal students as well and, consequently, a broader target system.

A proactive approach not only requires the examination of possible alternatives, but also the ability to predict future problems, needs, or issues. Forecasting requires assessing or predicting future conditions and anticipating the behavior of individuals and institutions under those conditions. Demographic projections, simulations, or econometric projections are used, along with the more conceptual approach of developing alternative scenarios.

An excellent example of this model is the efforts of social workers to achieve legal regulation of social work practice. Rather than reacting to public pressure regarding services for the poor from untrained workers, or to action by legislators that might encompass a multitude of disciplines under one regulatory structure, a proactive strategy has been developed. In the early 1970s, for example, NASW developed a model licensure bill which they promulgated nationally. Almost all state NASW chapters have modified this bill and over two-thirds have successfully lobbied for passage of some form of state legal regulation for social work practice. This effort and others like it have not only protected the quality of services to the public, but also have regulated service providers.

All of these approaches are used to try to project future needs, problems, or both. Developing policy requires a thoughtful examination of future conditions and needs, a realistic projection of future financial and technological resources, and an approach that accommodates these factors. Knowledge of how social institutions and organizations behave and change is needed also to anticipate organizational responses to particular policies.

What should be evident about a proactive orientation is its active approach to policy development, its eclectic sampling of a variety of policy models, and its reliance on a systems perspective. Although use of this approach requires finding reliable, current data to use in projecting future problems and needs, it encourages a posture of initiation rather than one of reaction.

POLICY EVALUATION

Introducing, negotiating, and implementing policies are important aspects of but do not complete the policy process. To make informed choices among policy alternatives, an ongoing evaluation of established policies is necessary.

Policy evaluation usually requires a review of programs that flow from the policy being reviewed. Consequently, you must be cautious about judging the merit of any policy on the basis of an examination of only one program. Although evaluation has inherent limitations, that arise from procedures such as generalizing findings, it is the authors' belief that policy evaluation is nonetheless superior to judgments made simply on the basis of political expediency, intuition, or organizational pragmatics. The merit of a particular program might be measured through examination of that one program, but the success of a particular policy is best determined by multiple program analyses.

Exclusive use of a single evaluation technique reduces, or narrows, the information that can be gathered about the topic under investigation. This may be necessary because of limitations on data, time, money, and the like, but it will skew in one direction the data collected and the resulting decisions. Consequently, an evaluation that incorporates multiple types of evaluation techniques may be more useful and is preferred, all other things being equal.

Effort   To focus on effort as the primary criteria by which to judge the success of a policy means to collect information about what it takes to deliver the policy in terms of staff, equipment, buildings, and so forth. The basic question, therefore, is "how much?"

Data related to effort include costs of salaries, equipment, fringe benefits, travel, rent, utilities, and supplies. Even such tangible costs sometimes are difficult to ascertain or estimate in multiprogram agencies, where proportions of all of the preceding expenses may be attributable to different programs in varying degrees.

Sometimes evaluations of effort may focus on the output of a program. In such instances, collecting data on units of service becomes important. Although this certainly provides information about the numbers of individuals served or the units of service produced, it alone does not measure the effects of a service. This caution is necessary because it is sometimes inferred that units of service produced equals success, or problems solved. That is, projected versus actual output of numbers of clients served often is presented to funders as a measure of success, even though such statistics do not indicate whether the clients' goals have been met or problems solved.

Quality As policies are translated into administrative regulations and procedures, quality control measures often are included. This may be done through separate legislation on accreditation or licensure. In either case, the basic thrust is similar: to evaluate the policy or program on the basis of the quality of services rendered.

Measures of quality focus not on "how much?" but rather on "what kind?" Indicators of a good program might include level of staff training, education, and experience; worker-to-client ratios; measures of worker performance; compliance with other accreditation measures specific to the program, such as the number of square feet per child in day care settings or a requirement that workers pass a statewide licensure examination. These are meaningful measures of the quality of any policy, but they may lead to inferences that the higher the quality of the program, the more successful the program or policy is. Often this is a questionable and untested assumption. These indicators are central to the analytic focus only if the policy was introduced primarily to enhance quality in specific programs. For example, if staff educational requirements were raised to enhance the quality of professional service, a measure of proportion of staff with higher degrees would be a reasonable indicator of increased quality.

Effectiveness A third approach to evaluation is to measure a policy's effectiveness. Utilizing this approach, the central question becomes "to what extent are the policy/program goals being met?" Although this approach comes nearest to measuring the "success" of a policy, the ability to collect information on program outcomes is certainly dependent on the ability to translate program/policy goals and objectives into measurable indicators of success. Ideally, it also requires the collection of preprogram as well as postprogram data.

This may be the most useful type of information about a policy's impact, but it also can be the most difficult to gather. Programs often operationalize shorter-term goals, leaving the achievement of the long-term policy goal to be inferred. For example, although the goal of detoxification may be to reduce alcohol consumption permanently, the measurable indicator may be taken at the point of termination from the program rather than several years later.

When it is impossible or too costly to collect, measurable data on program participants before and after their participation, aggregate statistics sometimes are employed. The reduction in teenage pregnancies as measured by health statistics may be used to evaluate the success of a high school course on birth control or the establishment of a local family planning clinic. In both cases, the inference of causality is untested and the conclusions, therefore, are based on circumstantial rather than direct evidence.

Efficiency When the primary focus of an evaluation is on cost relative to effectiveness, efficiency is the criterion being used. This type of analysis requires calculating per unit or per client costs for similar programs and consequently facilitates cross-program comparisons. For example, if effectiveness of goal attainment is held constant it would then be possible to compare a unit of adult day care, home-delivered meals, or adult residential nursing home care delivered by different programs.

The analysis might also include the use of cost-benefit techniques in which benefits are calculated in dollar terms. Thus, the evaluator cannot simply say that 60 percent of an elderly population served by a given nutrition program were properly nourished and maintained or improved in health status. Rather, the evaluator must be able to indicate the worth of this improved health status in dollars. Determining that state and federal governments spent less on Medicaid and Medicare reimbursements as a result of this program would involve translating governmental benefits into dollar terms.

It is even more complicated, but of equal importance, to be able to calculate what these benefits mean in dollar terms to the individual client and to the local community, as well as to the government. In the previous example, one might calculate the money saved by an individual client of a nutrition program in terms of lessened medical bills, or the money saved by the community in terms of unneeded ambulance or public health services.

Quite clearly, some benefits are more easily translated into dollars. Perhaps, as the illustrations suggest, one can estimate with some validity the amount of medical expenses saved. Other benefits, such as the saving of a life or prevention of a marital separation, are much more difficult to convert into financial equivalents.

CONCLUSION

An examination of a variety of policy models and evaluative strategies, can help one make the choice of appropriate political action in a more informed manner. Furthermore, by moving beyond theoretical models to prescriptions for professional practice, the practitioner increasingly can become aware of the linkage between and importance of both theory and practice. Theory and analysis, without subsequent prescriptions for practice, are of limited professional utility; wisdom gained through practice, without conceptual underpinnings, may be divorced from both long-term knowledge building and generalizations.

In summary, each of the models discussed in this chapter provides specific prescriptive tactics for political intervention. Further, they require skills and interventive strategies related to monitoring, lobbying, coalition building, and the entering of the legislative arena more directly through support of candidates and the holding of political office. These strategies will be described in the forthcoming chapters.

ASSIGNMENTS

A. Choose a current, newly enacted state policy.
   1. Use two of the models to analyze it.
   2. Identify a strategy for changing or modifying this policy as suggested by the model.
B. Identify a potential future problem.
   1. Predict the future extent of the problem.
   2. Describe the type of policy necessary to resolve the problem.
C. Choose a current state policy and analyze it through an efficiency criteria.
   1. Suggest ways of costing out benefits to client as well as to society.
   2. Describe elements you would include as costs in delivering policy.

SUGGESTED READINGS

Gil, David. "A Systematic Approach to Social Policy Analysis." *Social Service Review*, 44 (1970): 4, pp. 411–426.

Sosin, Michael, and Sharon Caulum. "Advocacy: A Conceptualization for Social Work Practice." *Social Work*, 28 (January–February 1983): 1, pp. 12–18.

REFERENCES

Dye, Thomas. *Understanding Public Policy*. New Jersey: Prentice-Hall, 1981.

Humberger, Edward. "A Political-Economic Approach to Human Services." Papers presented at the 1977 ASPA (American Society of Public Administration) National Conference. Washington, DC: Human Resources Administration, 1977.

Lindblom, Charles E. "The Science of Muddling Through." *Public Administration Review*, 19 (Spring 1959): pp. 79–88.

4
The Practitioner's Influence on Policy

The knowledge and skills students accumulate in social welfare policy and services should prepare them to exert leadership and influence as legislative and social advocates, lobbyists, and expert advisors to policy makers and administrators.

COUNCIL ON SOCIAL WORK EDUCATION
CURRICULUM POLICY STATEMENT, 1982

The general social work practitioner presumably is equipped with a framework and an array of roles that allow for intervention at the macro- as well as at the micro-level. Policy analysis, policy making, and political intervention must be a central part of this framework (Pierce, 1984).

As subsequent chapters point out, data on social problems or needs is absolutely crucial to effectiveness in political intervention. A lobbyist cannot sway a legislator on a piece of legislation on day-care, for example, without statistics, scenarios, or both, to back up the position, and the practitioner is the best source of such data, because the practitioner is on the front line. In contact with clients on a daily basis, the practitioner often develops particular insight into social problems as well as firsthand knowledge of the target population.

The purpose of this chapter is to emphasize the importance of the practitioner, both directly and indirectly, to an array of political activities. Practitioners can have tremendous impact on legislative, administrative, and fiscal decision making simply by utilizing their practice knowledge and clinical data.

It is unfortunate that all social work practitioners do not have within their repertoire of knowledge and skills an array of solutions to social problems, from case- or micro-level to political interventions. This would not

38

necessarily add additional tasks to the practitioner's role or require the learning of new skills, because the actions involved primarily consist of information dissemination and client empowerment strategies.

INFORMATION DISSEMINATION

Documentation Regardless of work setting, the practitioner continually encounters unmet needs, social problems, and gaps in or barriers to service. However, recognition of such needs and problems seldom results in collective, public activity by practitioners. More commonly, practitioners treating problems such as marital conflict, poor family communication, or parenting difficulties may look to a new treatment approach, read or write an article, or develop or attend a workshop. Macro-level solutions, such as changing a policy or program, or establishing a new program or agency, seem to come less readily to the practitioner's mind.

No matter what form of intervention a social worker may undertake, be it community organization, casework, administration, or political activity, the resource most needed and used is information. Before any diagnosis can be reached or community-organization strategy developed, information about the client's background and presenting problem or the community's problem and demographics must first be obtained. Intervention in the political arena has the same basic requirement, because the same processes are used by the social worker in the political arena as in case or community work.

Also important is the social worker's daily interaction with clients, not only for the purpose of data collection, but also to facilitate the organization or mobilization of clients in their own behalf, when necessary. The practitioner's relationship with clients or client groups provides clients with additional insight and motivation, both of which help to enable clients to advocate for themselves.

Social workers, practicing in a variety of settings (hospital, juvenile homes, the courts, public schools, mental health clinics, and so forth) are in a position to respond quickly and authoritatively when asked about the major difficulties they face in serving clients: lack of time to adequately help people, too large a case load, insufficient resources. Each practitioner is an expert on problems, needs, and resources. Clearly, therefore, the practitioner can become an ideal conduit between those who have problems and needs and those who are politically active. Unfortunately, this doesn't often occur, because the practitioner's knowledge and expertise usually remain at the case level. The missing link that would bridge the gap would be to aggregate individual practitioners' diagnoses and data into the kind of information that is necessary in order to function in the political sphere.

Increasingly, most agencies have some form of system by which to gather data that justifies expenditures to funding sources and describes activities to boards and to the community. Most of these information systems, whether simple and idiosyncratic to the program or highly complex or standardized, are usually constructed to depict or describe the activities of the staff (management information systems) or the characteristics and problems of the clients (client information systems). Consequently, even the most comprehensive and technical of these do not always identify unmet needs nor adequately illuminate the overlapping dimensions of a problem.

The practitioner can pull together case statistics and scenarios that clarify, expand, or redefine a problem area in ways that an information system cannot. For example, as the numbers of teen mothers who choose to keep their babies increases, public school policies need to be changed, if teen mothers are to continue their education. Working individually, practitioners might find individual solutions for each young mother, but because the problem is both a social and an individual one, social or political solutions such as public school policy changes also are needed. Thus, a major requirement of advocacy for policy change is documentation by practitioners of needed services (Briar & Briar, 1982).

Because information systems are initiated to serve either agency documentation or clinical diagnostic needs, it is not surprising that the use of these in political testimony, legislative support, or administrative rule writing and program implementation may appear to be an afterthought. However, as documentation is a primary step in any problem-solving process in social work, systems should be designed for multiple purposes, including clinical, administrative, and political activities. Social work staff at all levels should be able not only to input data but also to manipulate it to create categories and groupings that answer many questions, problems, and needs in various dimensions.

If practitioners become imbued with the idea that they have a unique and essential role in the documentation of needs, problems, and resources, they may find the task of "paper pushing" less cumbersome, boring, or unessential. Although their documentation skills and their information are essential to the political process, practitioners themselves do not need to be directly involved as political activists or advocates in order to contribute to political solutions.

Testimony   Given that legislators possess limited knowledge of the wide variety of subjects about which they must make decisions, testimony from the field is an essential part of political deliberations. Here is another opportunity for practitioners effectively to use their experience, expertise, skill, and knowledge to influence decisions made in the political arena.

Presentation at a legislative hearing of testimony using scenarios can have a major impact. Because the practitioner has access to clients who may be affected by a current or future policy, testimony can be enhanced by the inclusion not only of documented statistics, scenarios, and case illustrations, but also by the presence of clients themselves. The practitioner may speak on the client's behalf or have the clients speak for themselves. Either of these tactics can be used in a highly persuasive manner.

Of concern to the practitioner is the client's potential loss of confidentiality and anonymity through the use of client information, client profiles, case illustrations, and the client's presence. The social worker must be cautious about jeopardizing any individual client's privacy.

It is essential to keep in mind the basic principle of client self-determination when decisions are made about a client advocating on behalf of his or her own best interest or on the behalf of other clients. In fact, having the client take matters into his or her own hands to affect a solution is a recommended part of the helping process. Consequently, the role of enabler is an essential role for the social work practitioner. If not already aware of them, clients should be shown that it is possible to implement situational, environmental, political, and organizational solutions to problems as well as personal solutions. The introduction of macro-level solutions in turn helps to reinforce in clients the idea that their problems may not be caused by their own inadequacies.

Testimony by both the practitioner and the client is an extremely dynamic lobbying tool and is most dramatically done by the practitioners and clients directly affected. It may be more persuasive than the most expensive lobbyist who, after all, must rely on secondary sources, such as aggregate data or "secondhand" stories. Thus, the client or social worker who can present facts, personal vignettes, and scenarios, and who also is a constituent, can play a significant role for clients and in major policy settings—a role that no other individual or group can fill.

Expert Witness Legislative committees may request testimony or allow designated time slots for organizations and individuals to give testimony about an issue currently before that committee. Expert witnessess usually are called by invitation, and the expert must hold certain credentials— educational or experiential—to be deemed "expert." Sometimes legislators will undertake trips to seek information, witness events, or experience a particular social problem, so that they can themselves provide this firsthand type of information.

As noted in subsequent chapters, information is crucial to policy making. It is the practitioner who is the expert on many client needs and problems, far more than the social work administrator or the paid professional lobbyist. The role of expert usually excludes clients because the term often implies possession of specific educational credentials and a breadth of professional experience. Part of the verification of one's qualifications as an expert might include the ability to project the course of future events if a problem or need were to go unattended, and to show that these predictions have empirically demonstrable bases.

Although, as mentioned, the role of expert witness usually is undertaken at the invitation of a legislative or administrative group, social work practitioners could make themselves more visibly ready to undertake this role and better prepare themselves to serve as expert witnesses if asked.

Written Communication   Writing letters to legislators is another important professional role that practitioners can fill. Many don't realize the potential impact of one letter from a professional. Nor does letter writing take much work: legislators want to know as concisely as possible which bill one is writing about and the position taken; they want brief documentation for that position and enough identification so that the writer can be contacted for additional information. This type of letter is not difficult to write. Letter writing will be discussed more fully in Chapter 6 on lobbying.

Many human service organizations have newsletters or house organs that can and should routinely be disseminated to state and federal legislators and relevant decision makers. The potential pay-off in visibility for the organization, its clientele, and the services it provides is well worth the modest investment required. Increasing a public official's awareness of the services an organization provides is as important as is documentation of existing unmet needs. Both pieces of information are essential to informed decision making.

CLIENT EMPOWERMENT

Enabler/Advocate Role   Inherent in the general social work practitioner's functions is the role of enabler or advocate. One of the basic social work principles is to help clients move toward independence from the social worker, to enable clients to define and resolve their own problems, and to help them become self-advocates.

These roles require more than the collection of data and the consequent assessment of the situation or problem. They require the practitioner to imbue clients with the ability to "own" their problems and to identify client strengths for overcoming them. In the role of advocate, the practitioner moves from analysis to action requiring clients to identify resources and assert their rights.

Although the advocate role is most commonly utilized with individual clients, to move from case (individual) to class (group) advocacy requires no additional skills, other than the ability to aggregate data or mobilize clients. Community organizers build on these basic principles as a practice specialization, but specialization is not required.

Practitioners must not be so constrained by their therapeutic specialization or by an agency's policies on eligibility or service modalities that they become unable to see that macro-level problems require macro-level solutions. For example, if an elderly single person who is depressed because of isolation from the community and loss of independence is treated for depression, this may well represent an example of the inability to recognize macro-level solutions. The astute practitioner might also examine community resources to ascertain whether adult day care centers and accessible transportation are available. If not, he or she could query practitioners in similar agencies to see if a sufficiently large client group exists to warrant further strategies, and if so, advocate with them or on their behalf for the development of these services.

An additional benefit of enabling clients to advocate on their own behalf is that it not only gives clients a sense of ability to control their lives, but skills that are useful and transferable to various other situations.

Evaluator/Consultant Role Thus far we have discussed roles that include and activate clients, or involve workers on behalf of clients, to seek needed policies and services or to improve inadequate ones. Consequently, we have identified an array of roles, such as testifying and lobbying, that are linked to the external, often political, arena.

Practitioners also are in a central position to identify and evaluate the effects on their organizations of legislative policies and to determine whether the rule writing and implementation phases have been logically interpreted and consistently followed. Chapter 7 on monitoring will describe these processes in greater detail.

Once policies have been passed or services have been introduced or redesigned, the practitioner delivering those services is presumed to be the person best placed and qualified to act as an evaluator and consultant to determine whether new policies or services follow the intent of the legislation: Do the rules prescribe services that will overcome the barriers and issues articulated? Is access assured to the targeted client group? Are clients better off now that the service is available? This is not to suggest that agencies necessarily will invite or encourage this type of critique. However, it is a vital function in policy making and a logical role for the practitioner.

Voter Registration The central premise of the democratic process is that of freedom of individuals to choose among candidates who represent an array of political ideologies. Voting is the mechanism by which citizens have the opportunity to voice their opinions, make decisions, and elect those who shall represent them. Our system requires voters to be registered before they can vote in an election.

Promoting and enhancing client self-determination is a basic value of social work. Voting is one of the mechanisms that permit the citizens in a democratic nation to have a voice in determining the nation's domestic and foreign policies. Nonetheless, a large proportion of citizens are not even registered to vote, and not surprisingly, a disproportionate number of these unregistered voters are social work clients: the poor, the young, the elderly, the unskilled.

It is consistent with social work principles to assist clients to exercise their democratic right to self-determination. One way to do so is to help them register to vote. However, recent voter registration activities undertaken by social workers and schools of social work have been opposed by some members of the profession. They argue that registration is a partisan act and therefore is unlike other enabling activities, such as assisting clients to obtain a food stamp identification card, secure necessary documentation to rent an apartment, or file a death certificate so that insurance claims can be processed. Also, arguments have been made, often based on misconceptions about state Hatch acts, that public employees are prohibited from undertaking voter registration activity.

In reality, however, voter registration regulations are established by state statutes, and range from simple, accessible procedures to ones that are highly restricted and controlled. The more they are controlled by political parties, the more likely it is that voter registration will be viewed as a partisan activity even though state Hatch acts in fact mandate that coercion of employees on the job to support partisan candidates is prohibited. Consequently, voter registration activities are legitimate and essential components of the democratic process.

INFLUENCING POLICY: AN ILLUSTRATION

Mary, a social worker for a local community agency, has been involved for several months in the distribution of food to the unemployed and to others in need. Over the months, it became increasingly obvious to her that a large number of young people were coming in for food. She presented this observation at an agency staff meeting and a decision was made that the agency should begin to collect standardized data on the ages of clients, to see if Mary's observations had any significance.

After several months, data that had been collected showed a disproportionately high number of teenagers requesting food. Further exploration into agency records indicated that these teenagers were also parents. At a second staff meeting, a decision was made to gather additional statistics to determine the specific problems these teenage mothers were encountering.

Analysis of census data indicated that in the agency's service area, the birth rate was decreasing but the number of children born to teenage mothers had dramatically increased. Additional research revealed only a very few services were available to adequately address this population's needs.

Mary, looking for a program response from her agency, suggested that they start a teenage mothers' group to address emotional, personal, and environmental problems likely to be shared by teen mothers. When the agency advised some other referral sources that such a group was to be started, a flood of inquiries followed immediately and the program rapidly expanded.

However, a lack of resources caused the agency to limit the number of clients served by the new program. The agency's inability to meet the client demand was dramatized in an article in the agency's newsletter, which is routinely distributed to governmental officials and legislators. Almost immediately, Mary received an inquiry from an aide to one of the state senators. After discussions with the aide, Mary decided to organize a meeting of staff from a variety of agencies as well as interested individuals, to discuss the problems of teenage mothers and possible solutions to them. Her attendance list included not only the staff from the local community action center, the family service association, and the county welfare department, but also the senator's aide, public school officials, and a representative of the labor department.

The meeting resulted in the formation of a coalition to raise the consciousness of governmental agencies concerning this client group's need for services. A position paper developed by the coalition identified the dimensions of the need, explained that these families were at high risk, on a multitude of levels for child abuse, neglect, domestic violence, alcoholism, and poor family functioning, and projected the long-term costs of leaving these problems unattended. The paper was distributed to funding sources, legislators, and other key officials in order to alert them to this problem and ask for their support. Because the initial response was sparse, the coalition decided to broaden its base by identifying statewide groups dealing with child abuse, domestic violence, runaways, and related problems. These associations were enlisted in the agency's efforts to increase the awareness and attention of legislators. Together they formed a statewide coalition that began the same process—this time on a statewide level—of collecting data and researching the problem. Mary was now very busy developing groups for teenage mothers. She felt confident that her efforts had generated sufficient activity around this problem area, although she no longer was involved with the coalition.

When a public hearing was scheduled to review proposed legislation, Mary arranged for some of her teen-group members to travel to the state capital to testify about their concerns and their need for services. Presenting a group of teenage mothers to the committee proved highly effective in persuading the members to expedite the bill to the floor of the senate. A byproduct of the trip was that the young mothers felt that they had done something to help themselves. Being able to sway a group of legislators also made them feel somewhat powerful.

Mary asked the group of mothers if many of them had voted for the state senator who had chaired the committee, and she discovered that almost none of the group was registered to vote. Believing it would enhance her clients' empowerment if they were registered, Mary became a deputy of the city clerk and, at one of their group meetings, she registered all of the teenage mothers. She not only instilled self-confidence in her clients, but also gave them a channel through which they could express their concerns on election day.

Finally, enough pressure was brought to bear on the state legislature to get passed a budget-line item that provided funds to agencies for the purpose of addressing the multitude of teenage mothers' problems. Mary's efforts triggered a chain of events that ultimately led to a large-scale effort to meet client needs.

CONCLUSION

It should be evident that the practices and processes advocated throughout this chapter already are in place and part of the intrinsic fabric of social work. As with so many of the skills and techniques discussed in this book, they require only the ability of the social work professional to translate them from the micro- to the macro-level arena of practice.

Furthermore, we have seen that intervention in the policy or political arena need not be direct. Repackaging existing information in a slightly different manner and enlisting other individuals in coalition building or problem identification may be all that is necessary.

The empowerment of clients may be strategically utilized, or may occur as an outgrowth of other activities. In either case, it is a core social work principle, not an ancilliary function.

ASSIGNMENTS

1. Examine the client data collected by an agency where you are interning or to which you have access. Does the agency collect sufficient information to document a need for new services, policies, or both? If so, explain how. If not, what kinds of information would they need to collect?
2. Through observations made by you in your work with individual clients, generate two research questions that could be tested by having practitioners within the agency collect additional information.
3. Identify an unmet need among your client population and present a political strategy for filling this need. Describe the steps that are necessary steps in the process.

SUGGESTED READINGS

O'Connell, Brian. "From Service to Advocacy to Empowerment." *Social Casework*, 59 (April 1978): pp. 195–202.

Sunley, Robert. "Family Advocacy: From Case to Course." *Social Casework*, 51 (June 1970): pp. 347–357.

REFERENCES

Briar, Katherine Hooper, and Scott Briar. "Clinical Social Work and Public Policies." In *Practical Politics: Social Work and Political Responsibility* by Maryann Mahaffey and John Hanks (Eds.), Washington DC: National Association of Social Workers, 1982, pp. 45–54.

Pierce, Dean. *Policy for the Social Work Practitioner*. White Plains, NY: Longman, 1984.

5
Political Action Committees

Although social reform and client advocacy traditionally have been viewed as legitimate aspects of social work methodology, organized efforts at political reform by social workers are recent. It might seem self-evident that social workers would need to become politically active in order to effect political reform. Certainly those who have been politically active have done so through such initiatives as testifying, letter writing, or lobbying. It is our contention, however, that collective efforts will prove more effective than individual efforts. For that reason, we endorse political action committees (PACs) as an important and powerful method for affecting social policy and social change.

PACs are organizations designed to collect and disperse voluntary contributions for political purposes from members of a special interest group. In order to meet state and federal regulations, they must be independently organized and funded.

Political action committees vary because state election laws differ. Generally a PAC is organized specifically to offer financial support to candidates, to raise funds for donation, and to urge the PAC membership as well as the general public to support candidates endorsed by the parent organization. Special interest groups (business, labor, professional associations, corporate employees) coordinate and systematize these efforts to support candidates viewed as sympathetic to that particular special interest group's positions.

Although PACs are organized primarily to provide financial support to candidates, they influence policy in other ways as well, particularly through coalition building and education and skill development of PAC members. PACs are important to candidates who need and value endorsements and financial contributions when they are up for election or re-election. Conversely, the parent organization assumes that receiving assistance from a political action committee may lead a potential legislator, for example, to be increasingly supportive of the PAC's positions in the future (Abrams & Goldstein, 1981). Finally, the principle of collectively organizing to endorse candidates suggests that the support generated will be larger than that given by any single individual and more visible to the candidate.

PACs have been in existence since 1972. The recent proliferation of PACs is striking, and the current total of 3000 business and labor PACs reflects an estimated 60 percent increase in the last eight years (Hunt, 1982). Not only have the number of PACs increased, but the amount of money contributed by PACs to congressional election campaigns has been estimated at well over $80 million, a significant increase from $55 million contributed in 1980 and $12.5 million in 1974.

Particularly since the recent growth of PACs, controversy has arisen about the negative aspects of "vote buying". Consequently, there has been debate about changing state and federal election laws to limit PAC maximum contributions to candidates or to prohibit them entirely.

In keeping with the national trend, in 1976 the National Association of Social Workers created a PAC called Political Action for Candidate Election (PACE) in order to offer financial support to candidates at the federal level. Florida became the first state to create a state-level NASW Political Action Committee, followed soon after by Michigan, California, and Indiana. To be sure, NASW PACs may be slightly different from those sponsored by business and industry. Social work PACs, for example, may not have the financial resources available to other PACs, but this handicap often can be balanced by social workers' skill in interpersonal relationships, community organization, and volunteer action.

To those potential PACE members who say that social workers should not form PACs, it can be argued that many other groups that have developed PACs and utilized them effectively support positions diametrically opposed to NASW positions.

Table 5.1 compares the top fund-raising PACs with NASW PACs. It may be assumed that affluent PACs will assure that candidates are elected who are sympathetic to particular goals. During debate in Congress over three proposed national health insurance plans, for example, the American Medical Association (AMA) and NASW took very different positions. Poor people, sick people, the elderly, and children do not make political campaign contributions, and indeed, often don't or can't vote. Thus, a social workers' PAC is a necessary advocacy group, not only for professional self-interest and protection, but for the disadvantaged and disenfranchised as well.

Political action committees eventually may come under greater scrutiny and, perhaps, more legislative regulation and monitoring, but until that time, they are a significant force in the electoral process. In order for human service workers to be able to influence the sweeping antihuman service movement, they also must participate in the process.

This chapter will explore in depth why PACs are organized, how they are utilized in candidate selection and endorsement, and the targeting strategies useful in distributing available resources.

WHY IS A PAC ORGANIZED?

Those most critical of political action committees say they are organized only to purchase votes from candidates. In reality, there are important reasons for the formation of a PAC: (1) to provide information about candidates and issues to members, and (2) to better utilize resources. More specifically, this means that a PAC can help individuals keep abreast of the positions represented by various congressional, state, and local candidates, thus enabling them to determine what effect the election of each of these candidates may have on the special interest group.

TABLE 5.1 Business and Professional PACs

Receipts in the 1981–1982 Election Cycle	
American Medical Assn.	$1,842,026
National Assn. of Realtors	1,570,158
American Medical Assn. (Calif.)	1,152,568
American Medical Assn. (Texas)	819,331
National Automobile Dealers Assn.	752,373
National Assn. of Home Builders	705,941
National Assn. of Life Underwriters	671,787
American Bankers Assn.	556,149
American Dental Assn.	553,175
Chicago Mercantile Exchange	538,531
American Medical Assn. (Florida)	487,205
Assn. of Trial Lawyers of America	459,598
Associated General Contractors of America	438,246
Independent Insurance Agents of America	328,187
Social Work PACs	
National Assn. of Social Workers	130,000
NASW Massachusetts	12,000
NASW Michigan	10,550
NASW Indiana	3,550
NASW California	1,600

Source: Information gathered from the Federal Elections Commission and from chairpersons of state NASW PACs.

Further, a PAC can alleviate the indecision that may arise when one attempts to determine how best to use one's own resources (time, skills, money) on behalf of candidate support. This indecision often is compounded by the geographic distance between candidates and the individual and by the fact that an individual's resources seldom are sufficient on their own to have substantial impact on a campaign or a candidate. A candidate is far more likely to remember the contribution of a group whose endorsement represents approval of his or her policies than a number of smaller contributions from several constituents. Furthermore, unlike most individuals, a PAC usually endorses and contributes to many candidates, so its potential influence extends to a much larger segment of the total legislative body than does that of one individual.

The main objective of a PAC is to elect candidates who favor its policies and positions. The many strategies used to accomplish this goal will be discussed later. The resulting actions have several anticipated consequences, the most important of which is to gain a politician's attention after election. Also, because politicians need to be informed about many issues in order to govern effectively, they value people and organizations who can provide them with reliable information. Therefore, the provision and dissemination of information concerning current legislative issues is a central function of one division of NASW—the Education and Legislative Action Network (ELAN). ELAN was developed six years before PACE, for the purpose of determining professional positions on current legislative issues, collecting supportive documentation, and lobbying. Now PACE and ELAN work together to develop social policy for both organizations.

Once a candidate sympathetic to a PAC's positions is elected, his or her political appointment of special interest group members is of obvious benefit in furthering the group's goals. A governor, for example, may make as many as 2000 appointments, some of which will undoubtedly affect social policy.

PROCESS OF SELECTION

Because it is not unusual for a political candidate to slant his or her position on a particular issue in order to gain the support of specific groups, often it becomes necessary to determine how a politician really stands on issues that may not be of major campaign interest. In the case of incumbents, the best measurement is action already taken. Consequently, to give a clearer picture of the candidates' positions on those issues, PACs often prepare and publicize a record of the candidate's votes on relevant pieces of legislation— sometimes referred to as the "report card."

In the course of a legislative session, a legislator may cast hundreds of votes. Many of the votes may run along party lines as indications of party support; other votes may be on procedural issues or minor amendments to a bill. These votes are not good indications of position, although procedural votes (e.g., to table a bill) are used as indicators of position when there are no other bills related to a particular issue to monitor. For example, although a vote to legalize abortion is not taken regularly, votes on legislation dealing with physicians' regulations on providing an abortion may provide a barometric measure of the candidate's position.

Not all legislation will be equally important to a particular PAC. A PAC representing social workers, for instance, is not interested in a candidate's position on materials used in highway construction, but would be interested in the candidate's position on a nursing home bill of rights or medicaid co-payment. Clearly, the first step is to choose the issues to be used in developing the "report card." Given the great number of votes taken in a legislative session, this is a challenging task. Usually a PAC chooses a limited number of bills that correspond with the organization's goals. Then the records are reviewed to determine the candidate's vote on each issue, noting whether the candidate voted for or against the organization's position (see Table 5.2).

As Table 5.2 illustrates, a further decision must be made in the analysis of the voting record: how to count absences. For example, Senator Heflin,

TABLE 5.2 Report Card of Selected Senate Incumbents

State	Senator	1	2	3	4	5	6	7	8	9	10	R	W
Alabama	Denton	W	W	W	W	W	W	W	W	W	W	0	10
	Heflin	R	W	R	W	R	–	–	W	W	W	3	5
Arizona	Goldwater	W	W	W	W	W	W	W	W	W	W	0	10
	DeCencini	R	W	R	W	R	W	W	–	R	R	5	4
Idaho	McClure	W	W	W	W	W	W	W	W	W	W	0	10
	Symms	W	W	W	W	W	W	W	W	W	W	0	10
Louisiana	Johnston	W	W	R	W	R	W	R	—	R	W	4	5
	Long	R	W	R	W	R	W	–	W	R	W	4	5
Massachusetts	Kennedy	R	R	R	R	R	R	R	R	R	R	10	0
	Tsongas	R	R	R	R	R	R	R	R	–	R	9	0
Michigan	Levin	R	R	R	R	R	R	R	R	R	R	10	0
	Riegle	R	R	R	R	R	R	R	–	R	R	9	0
Pennsylvania	Heinz	W	R	R	W	W	W	R	R	R	R	6	4
	Spector	W	R	R	W	W	R	R	R	W	R	6	4

1. School lunches
2. Urban-oriented programs
3. Legal Services Corporation
4. Transfer amendment
5. Social security
6. Abortion
7. Child nutrition
8. Food stamps
9. Child welfare
10. Rape victims

Source: 1981 Congressional Voting Records ELAN ALERT, NASW Legislative Department, 1981

Alabama, has record of 3 in favor and 5 opposed, but 2 absences on the 10 selected NASW issues. Many PACs would consider the absences as negative votes, presuming that an effective senator is one who votes. Before reaching this conclusion, however, it would be prudent to investigate the reason for the absences. After all, the legislator who is absent may have been working diligently on issues in his or her home district, or may have been ill.

The voting record is a helpful device when dealing with incumbents, but it does not represent the entire record. Other information, such as legislation sponsorship, can assist PAC members. Here caution must be used, because many legislators sponsor bills they know will die in committee, in order to secure political support or appease constituents or special interest groups. Committee votes and activities also may be important, because legislation of interest to the PAC may never reach a floor vote. Other matters to be investigated include the politician's committee assignments and his or her relative power within the legislative body. Consequently, a social work PAC would want to endorse a candidate who chairs the social services committee, if that politician's positions are acceptable within the PAC's limits.

Of course, some nonincumbents might be stronger supporters of human service issues than incumbent legislators. Obtaining an understanding of a nonincumbent's position is even more difficult. Often, it must be obtained by using a questionnaire, an interview or both. A questionnaire (see Table 5.3) can be open ended, dealing with the candidate's general philosophy, or closed, to identify his or her position on a specific issue or bill, such as the appropriate level of AFDC allowances. The nonincumbent's responses to the questionnaire or interview then must be compared to the record of his or her opponent.

The process of selection is not without complicating factors. A PAC must deal with many political realities, including the fact that in many political districts it is impossible to find a candidate who is totally supportive of the views of the PAC membership. Table 5.4 lists the proportion of Republican and Democratic voters in hypothetical districts. This data may be used in deciding which candidate to target in districts that are proportionally unfavorable to the candidate's party.

Clearly, there are times and circumstances when a PAC will endorse a candidate who, on the basis of his or her voting record, questionnaire, or interview, is not the ideal choice. For example, a PAC might endorse a candidate primarily because he or she is running against a number of candidates whose voting record is known to be unfavorable to human services, or an incumbent who has a marginal voting record on issues of concern to the PAC but who is considered a "shoe-in." In the latter case, it probably would be wise to endorse and provide at least some support to that candidate. This issue will be further explored later in this chapter.

A different type of dilemma exists when all the contending candidates support PAC policies and therefore are considered to be good potential legislators. In this situation PACs will not endorse any candidate for fear of alien-

TABLE 5.3 Selected Items from PAC Candidate Questionnaires

1. The Reagan administration has introduced a plan for a New Federalism that would shift responsibility for AFDC, Food Stamps, and other social programs to the states. Do you
   _____ Support the proposal in its present form?
   _____ Support the concept, but not for AFDC and Food Stamps?
   _____ Disagree with the concept?

2. Among Reagan's many federal deregulation proposals are ones that threaten the quality and quantity of health care services by decreasing the number of social work positions in existence. Which of the following best states your viewpoint?
   _____ Deregulation is necessary to achieve cost-effective health care.
   _____ The loss of the quality of services is of more concern to me than the potential cost saving.
   _____ The availability of services should be determined by the state rather than by the federal government.

3. What, in your view, are the most important problems facing our state?

4. A number of controversial social issues are being discussed now, some of which will come up in the next legislative session. Regardless of what you personally believe about these issues, how will you vote concerning public policy on the issues below?
   a. Because the right to choose abortion is based on a U.S. Supreme Court ruling, will you support Medicaid funding to pay for abortions?
      Yes _____ No _____
   b. If a bill permitting prayer in the public schools is reported to the floor of the Michigan legislature, how will you vote?
      Yes_____ No _____
   c. When the U.S. Constitutional amendment guaranteeing equal rights for women is submitted to the state for ratification, how will you vote?
      Yes _____ No _____

5. Do you feel that a family of two can meet necessary expenditures on $290.00 per month?
   Yes _____ No _____
6. What is your position on licensure of professionals?

Source: Questions 1 and 2 are from NASW's 1980 PACE questionnaire. Questions 3–6 are from Michigan's 1982 NASW M–PACE questionnaire.

ating the others who also have taken positions that are favorable to the organization.

An example of the difficulties a PAC may have in a primary race can be illustrated by the 1982 primary in Michigan's solidly Democratic Seventeenth Congressional District. Of seven candidates who ran in the primary, three were considered to be both very liberal and front runners, including Detroit City Councilwoman Maryann Mahaffey. The national NASW PAC endorsed Mahaffey because she was considered the best candidate and because she was a past president of NASW. The situation was difficult for many other PACs because their members viewed several of the candidates as potentially acceptable. Therefore, many of these PACs made no endorsement, and Mahaffey

TABLE 5.4 Proportion of Registered Republicans and Democrats by Districts (Hypothetical)

District	% Registered Republicans	% Registered Democrats
1	60	40
2	50	50
3	25	75
4	10	90

lost the election. Although other complicating factors were relevant to her loss, lack of PAC support was one.

Nonendorsement occurs frequently during primaries. Although many people feel that primaries are useless, many important decisions are made at this level. Winning the primary in some districts, for example, the Democratic nomination in District 4 in Table 5.4, is tantamount to being elected. Unfortunately, as important as the primaries are, voter turnout historically has been lower for primaries than for general elections.

CANDIDATE ENDORSEMENTS

Before discussing the variety of candidate endorsements available to a PAC membership, it should be noted that, generally, the earlier an endorsement is made, the greater the effect a PAC will have on the campaign. A candidate remembers those who helped create the momentum of his or her campaign. Early money, volunteers, and other support may deter competition, create a "winning attitude" for the chosen candidate, or both, which often induces other PACs to join the campaign. Senator Don Riegle, D., Michigan, told the NASW PACE Michigan representative that the $1000 received 16 months before a general election had the same effect as $7000 received 2 months before the election. Volunteers who join campaigns early have a far greater opportunity to affect policy issues and play a key campaign role. The benefit of an early endorsement is reciprocal, because many candidates will place the endorsements of the sponsoring organization on their campaign literature, thus enhancing the PAC's ability to raise money.

One argument in favor of late endorsements, however, should be acknowledged. The longer a PAC remains neutral in a given race, the more valuable the PAC's endorsement may become, thus increasing the PAC's ability to obtain the candidate's support for the PAC's position on critical issues. The larger the PAC the more effective this technique.

After a PAC committee has gathered and reviewed data on all candidates in a particular race, members must decide not only whom to endorse, but how. There are several ways in which an endorsement can be made:

1. The PAC can endorse the candidate by merely stating that the membership organization (for example, NASW) recommends that social workers vote for that candidate. Even though this is the simplest endorsement, it is perhaps least effective from the standpoint of the long-term objectives of the PAC.

2. Services and support can be offered, including mailing and telephone lists. Candidates are aware that the endorsement alone will not guarantee membership votes, but mailing lists and telephone numbers facilitate the candidate's ability to reach PAC members and to gain their support and labor.

3. A PAC can recruit and assign volunteers from its membership to assist candidates, thereby increasing the effect of the endorsement. Social workers' PACs (PACE) have found this to be most effective, because candidates have discovered that social workers have excellent campaign skills. Social workers listen well, are organized, are trained to take a broad perspective, and can work well with a variety of individuals (Wolk, 1981). Some candidates enlist social workers as campaign managers. Also, after an election, social workers often are hired as aides to work out constituent problems.

4. The most important form of support is financial. Campaigns are expensive, and financial support allows the candidate to mold his or her campaign to the community. As mentioned earlier, not all PAC-endorsed candidates receive financial support, but targeting candidates for in-kind as well as financial support is a more cost-efficient resource utilization method. Many PACs with considerable financial resources provide elaborate in-kind services to a candidate because the Federal Election Commission has set limits on the amount of money a PAC can contribute to a campaign. For example, the National Conservative Foundation, a sister organization of the National Conservative Political Action Committee (NCPAC), sponsors regional campaign schools. Students are charged a fee only if they are formally connected to a political campaign, and graduates are recommended to conservative candidates across the country. Additionally, NCPAC occasionally donates the in-kind services of a campaign manager to a particular candidate. Other PACs have supplied candidates with office space, telephone services, mailing equipment, and the like.

TARGETING

A PAC develops a targeting strategy in order to utilize resources most effectively. Obviously, it is relatively ineffective to contribute $5000 to a candidate who already has more financial support than is needed to run his or her campaign or who has little opposition. In order to target available resources effectively, a PAC must develop policy guidelines.

In developing a targeting strategy, the PAC first reviews the full range of political offices open in the upcoming elections and determines who is likely to be easily reelected or elected. Indeed, many incumbents do not campaign because they already have strong support or no opposition. Whether or not these obvious winners support human services, their races are not targeted because the outcome cannot be changed. The remaining races are examined for candidate compatibility with the PAC's positions. Each race is then reviewed to determine whether the PAC's efforts can have an effect on the outcome, and what amount of effort would be required for success. Typical guidelines for a PAC include the following:

1. Targeting supportive incumbent candidates who are in difficulty.
2. Targeting candidates who have the best chance of replacing an incumbent who does not support the PAC's interests.
3. Eliminating incumbents in leadership positions who are opposed to the organization's views on relevant issues.

Another form of targeting is known as "candidate development." This is a strategy by which individuals who are interested in running for office, and who support a PAC's goals and objectives, are helped to develop knowledge of issues and campaign skills. Locating a prospective candidate in a district that offers the best chance for success can be effective. The PAC then supplies the candidate with the maximum amount of financial support permitted and as much in-kind and volunteer support as possible.

NCPAC, for example, specifically engaged in candidate development with blacks in order to change many of the black districts from liberal to conservative. Further, social workers are beginning to develop candidates by prioritizing social workers for endorsement and financial support. Nancy Humphreys, past president of NASW, and Director, Michigan State University School of Social Work, hosted an institute to develop a curriculum for MSW programs that would enable social workers to compete in the political arena through presenting content on the political process, campaigning, and lobbying. Social workers would be encouraged to consider politics as a practical career specialization (Curriculum Development Institute, 1984).

Targeting strategies may be changed, eliminated, or reinstated during a campaign. For example, early in the 1982 senatorial race NASW's political action committee endorsed Senator Riegle of Michigan, in part because he had been targeted for defeat by NCPAC. The NASW PAC expected Michigan's popular Republican Governor Millikin to be his opponent. The social workers' PAC also contributed financially to the Riegle campaign. After the election the PAC speculated that early targeting and endorsement had helped to change the situation: NCPAC decided its money could be more wisely donated and the incumbent governor decided to retire.

FALL OUT

The greatest danger to a PAC is "fall out"—quarrelling and disagreement. Whenever a decision or action is taken for a large group of people, there will be those who fall out, and PACs must take this into consideration when making decisions to support candidates whose positions on the issues are not completely satisfactory. A PAC must weigh a politically advantageous decision against the potential loss of membership support. Obviously, losing membership contributions will decrease the PAC's effectiveness, but public quarrelling or overt support for the opposition are even more divisive, and not only will decrease the impact of the PAC's endorsement, but, more important, may become a wedge that could splinter the organization.

Within the human service profession, concern often is expressed about partisan politics. Historically, Democrats have tended to support human services and social work PACs frequently have found themselves endorsing Democratic candidates only. However, because many social workers are uncomfortable with the idea of a PAC that exclusively endorses candidates of one party, some social work PACs have sought Republican social workers to serve as PAC board members, thus assuring a nonpartisan ideology. Most important, however, is to endorse and elect pro—human service candidates, irrespective of party.

The need to make endorsements early may prevent or hamper a PAC's ability to weigh member dissent. Because many members are not politically active until campaigns are well underway, awaiting input from the total membership is often inimical to quick decision making. A PAC must take immediate action in an uncertain and risky environment, and often doesn't have time to poll the entire membership. The case of an incumbent candidate who decided to retire just before the primary presents an interesting example. He was an influential legislator with an adequate pro—human service record and his reelection appeared imminent. This created an excellent opportunity for the PAC to support a pro—human service candidate in an open race, but the urgency of the event made it imperative to make an immediate endorsement, thus risking member fall out.

IDEALISM VERSUS WINNING

A political action committee often must choose between a candidate whose philosophical beliefs are compatible with those of the PAC but who has a poor chance of winning, and a candidate members can "live with" who has a good chance of winning. The wrong endorsement decision in this scenario may determine whether the PAC has a political friend to work with, educate, and influence, or an enemy who does not wish to talk or listen. Also, it is in these situations that fall out from membership potentially can be most severe.

In these situations, the PAC must choose between idealism (the best candidate) versus winning (the most likely candidate). Figure 5.1 illustrates a continuum of 14 gubernatorial candidates in a state primary. Candidates are arrayed from left (prohuman services) to right (antihuman) services. Candidate A, who most closely agrees with social workers' positions, has run several times but has never gained a substantial proportion of the primary vote. A state senator, Candidate B, also favorable to social work policy issues, received the Citizen of the Year award from that state's NASW chapter and also was chair of the Senate Social Service Committee. However, he had done poorly both in the polls and in fundraising. The PAC felt it would be most advantageous to reelect him as senator, who would then retain his committee chairship. On the other hand, Congressman J, a six-term congressman with a 50 percent correct voting record, had been instrumental in developing legislation to pool the efforts of union and management in order to save a major corporation. He was perceived by the PAC to be a winner, and was favored in the polls. His organizational and campaign techniques appeared to be professional. Because an early endorsement was important, the PAC decided to endorse Congressman J, although some social workers already were engaged in senator B's campaign. Senator B pulled less than 5 percent of the primary vote and Congressman J received 50 percent, eventually winning the general election. Thus, the fact that a winner was chosen early ultimately resulted in an ideal candidate for the PAC, because early endorsement allowed access and time to educate the candidate on human services issues.

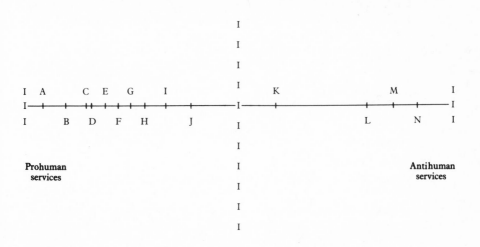

Figure 5.1 Primary gubernatorial rankings on human services issues.

CONCLUSION

It should be clear that the purpose of a PAC is to financially support candidates who have been or will be supportive of the PAC's position on specific issues. Because this may be construed as "vote buying," some concern exists about the legitimacy of the process. Nonetheless, PACs have proliferated and are contributing substantial dollars to political campaigns. Thus, social workers should be concerned that poor people and people who are in difficult circumstances and do not make campaign contributions also are represented.

The social work literature generally has been critical of political involvement by the social work profession and by social workers individually. Although a recent study concluded that social workers participate in the political arena as actively as any profession expects from its members (Wolk, 1981), political activity measured for the study included only traditional, individual methods such as letter writing and testifying. Collective political action and advocacy, although certainly consistent with basic social work goals, seems to have been overlooked and underutilized to date.

Decision-making procedures that determine endorsements may at times run counter to basic social work morals and ethics. Also, lobbying, campaigning, and recruiting voters may require skills and tactics not generally taught within social work education programs; tactics used by PACs may contradict the conventional social work principles of neutrality and client self-determination.

The major purpose of the national NASW PACE is to achieve legislative successes in the formation of social policy. As long as other special interest groups exert influence, NASW must accept the responsibility to become more assertive on behalf of its clients. That assertiveness, it can be argued, will be successful only through organized and collective political participation.

ASSIGNMENTS

A. Obtain two "report cards"—one from a social work PAC and one from another PAC.
    1. Identify any special interest legislation either PAC has chosen in order to examine the legislators' voting records.
    2. Review your state and federal legislators' records.
    3. Determine whether your legislator would be supported by either group and why.
B. Volunteer to work on a campaign (during an election year) or for a legislator who has been identified as being pro—human services.
    1. Identify the process by which a legislator is made aware of constitu-

ent issues, such as letters from constituents, pressures from a political party, and so forth.
2. Identify important constituent issues.
3. What is the legislator's response?

C. For your local, state, or federal legislator, obtain from an election commission the amount and source of financial contributions donated during the legislator's most recent campaign. Then compare the voting record of this legislator with the sources of contributions to his or her campaign. Does any evidence of "vote buying" exist? If so, document it and note what might be the most effective way of utilizing this information.

SUGGESTED READINGS

Abrams, Harvey, and Sheldon Goldstein. "A State's Comprehensive Political Program." In Maryann Mahaffey and John W. Hanks (Eds.), *Practical Politics: Social Work and Political Responsibility*. Washington, DC: National Association of Social Workers, 1981.

Ribicoff, Abraham. "Politics and Social Workers." *Social Work*, 7 (April 1962): pp. 3–6.

Wolk, James L. "Are Social Workers Politically Active?" *Social Work*, 26 (July 1981): pp. 283–288.

REFERENCES

Abrams, Harvey, and Sheldon Goldstein. "A State Chapter's Comprehensive Political Program." In Maryann Mahaffey and John W. Hanks (Eds.), *Practical Politics: Social Work and Political Responsibility*. Washington, DC: National Association of Social Workers, 1981, pp. 241–260.

Curriculum Development Institute, Michigan State University, East Lansing, MI: December 1984.

Hunt, Albert. "Special Interest Money Increasingly Influences What Congress Enacts." *Wall Street Journal* (July 1982): p. 7.

Wolk, James L. "Are Social Workers Politically Active?" *Social Work*, 26 (July 1981): pp. 283–288.

6
Influence through Lobbying

In a smoke-filled back room of a restaurant directly across the street from the capitol, a group of legislators continue a debate started earlier in committee hearings. The unresolved issue they are discussing is whether to appropriate additional revenues for services to learning-disabled children or for highway repair and reconstruction.

Several legislators believe learning-disabled children do not deserve special services. In their opinion, the problem of these children is laziness and inattentiveness and therefore the educational system should deal with it as a disciplinary problem. Others believe the money would be better spent on highway and road repair—a significantly more visible project that would affect all constituents.

A lone voice among the group speaks in support of appropriating the funds to the learning disabled, citing physical disabilities as well as difficult home environments. When asked why he takes this position, the legislator describes a child who lives next door to him who has a learning disability and tells how the parents are struggling to pay for private tutors and services.

The others conclude that this is only one example and may be the exception, not the rule. None of the legislators seem to know exactly how many other learning-disabled children are in the state or what problems they and their families face.

Earlier, a lobbyist for the highway repair appropriations bill had persuasively demonstrated the degree of popular concern for this legislation, and the number of complaints received about present conditions, and had argued the cost effectiveness of undertaking these projects now rather than waiting until the next legislative session. The lone legislator sympathetic to the learning disableds' cause, on the other hand, reluctantly admits that he does not know the extent of need and does not have significant constituent support for the proposal. In the absence of additional information or persuasive advocacy, and in light of the legislators' indifference to and ignorance of learning disabilities, the group supports the highway repair bill.

In the real world of political processes, decisions are influenced and made by those who work the system in their favor. This chapter will discuss what is commonly known as "politicking," or as it is more professionally termed, *lobbying*.

The term *politicking* is used frequently and indiscriminately. It is sometimes used as a personal adjective: "He (she) is really political." Unfortunately, this usually suggests that the individual is attempting to make contacts and influence individuals in order to enhance his or her own position. This may give negative connotations to politicking, suggesting that it is selfish and possibly underhanded.

Indeed, lobbing presumes the persuasive presentation of one side of an issue, primarily to influence decision makers. Because of this, many people, especially social workers, may refuse to participate in what may be viewed as selfish, untruthful, or conflicting practices. However, the American system of government was constructed on the notion of pluralism. In other words, it was designed to encourage and accommodate the expression of conflicting views, group conflict, negotiation, bargaining, and compromise. Lobbying is not a straightforward presentation of all positions on an issue, nor does it have as a goal the enhancement of influence or position. It is our contention that lobbying is a legitimate, fundamental, and powerful practice in a pluralistic society, and that social workers and their clients will continue to lose politically if they do not enter this arena.

Social workers often perceive lobbyists as representatives of special interest groups, failing to realize that they themselves are a special interest group also, with beliefs and values that prescribe goals and positions. Unlike other groups, however, the special interest of social workers always has been society's disadvantaged and disenfranchised members. Thus, the social work profession's special interest is not self-interest, but rather a concern for individuals, groups, and communities who cannot lobby for themselves.

For example, when President Reagan announced in 1979 that the private sector should fill the gap in human service revenues resulting from reduced federal support, no group was in a better position to lobby against this view than were social workers. Yet social workers took little collective action. Although clients of human services certainly have an interest in continuing services, they usually are not organized, knowledgeable, or articulate enough to lobby for themselves.

There are myths about the political process that often discourage social workers from participating in it. One myth is that social workers need specialized training in the political process before they can intervene. They fail to recognize the value of their knowledge and understanding of a community, of individuals, of an individual's functioning within the community, and of group interactions, but this knowledge is the most valuable tool that a social worker can bring to the lobbying process.

Another myth is that a large group of individuals with a lot of money is needed to influence legislators. In fact, there are numerous ways by which a single individual or a few individuals, with the right timing and the right information, successfully can affect social policy. Although it may dishearten many social workers to oppose groups with more resources and money, it should not be cause for retreat.

SOCIAL WORK SKILLS IN THE POLITICAL PROCESS

Because our political structure is both representative and pluralistic, it requires and even demands that some individuals speak on behalf of others, and that opposing groups resolve conflicts. The very nature of the political process is one of individual interaction, and this clearly implies the importance of social work skills.

Social workers are trained to understand how individuals relate and interact, how groups form and change, how miscommunications can alienate people from each other and from society, and how motivation affects behavior. Social workers can use this knowledge and their corresponding skills to understand and to intervene in the political process.

In the committee process, for example, a social worker who has background information on the committee members (such as district composition, the members' previous voting records, education, training, and previous professional experience) then can observe and understand committee member interactions. In many cases, the social worker subsequently would be able to predict what approach and what factors may persuade a given legislator to suuport the social workers' position. Social workers also receive training in in-depth, one-on-one interaction. These skills are certainly transferable to interactions with legislators. Equally important are the other basics of social work, such as knowledge of social problems, social interaction, and the social environment. This knowledge can be very beneficial to the legislator in the difficult task of legislative decision making.

It should be noted that at certain times and in some situations, the fact that a social worker is not a regular lobbyist can work in favor of influencing a legislator. This is so because the legislator will know that the social worker is lobbying because he or she is truly concerned, has a special interest, and is knowledgeable—and not because he or she is either being paid to lobby or acting out of self-interest. This should not suggest, however, that it is not important for social workers to build and maintain continuing relationships with legislators.

Throughout this book, we indicate the distinct importance of social work values. It bears repeating that the fact that social workers as lobbyists are less self-interested than are many other special interest groups may be an extremely influential factor. Some have charged that lobbying by social workers to continue or to implement a program is self-serving because such a program would create or maintain jobs for social workers. This argument should not be allowed to cloud the issue. The main reason for lobbying for programs is to provide needed services to people.

THE POLITICAL PROCESS

A formal process exists by which all legislation must proceed. Legislators must follow rules, regulations, and procedures before a bill finally can be voted on and passed to the executive branch. This procedure includes checks and balances to ensure input from multiple sources and conflict resolution between groups. The essence of the legislative process is making choices between conflicting objectives. Coming to a compromise on a specific piece of legislation can be an extremely time-consuming process. It is true that sometimes a bill can pass through Congress or a state legislature with lightning speed, but usually these are bills that either respond to very critical situations or have great public support.

To effectively influence legislation, social workers must understand precisely how the legislative process works. Each state has its own rules or procedures; the state printing office or state chamber of commerce will have this information or know where it can be obtained.

In general, legislative bodies are composed of committees, each with a separate jurisdiction and substantive area. It is in the committee that a bill is given its most thorough review or reading. A primary method by which committees obtain information is from public testimony; thus, the committee is a key public access point. One individual who acts at the right time with precise and persuasive information can have a tremendous effect on the committee process.

However, there are inherent problems with this process. First, committee agendas can change without notice. Second, committee meetings can be cancelled without notice. Third, bills sometimes are not placed on the committee agenda at all. One must keep informed about committee activity and be ready to counteract these problems.

The key person in the committee quite obviously is the chairperson. He or she has sole discretion over the committee and can choose to present a bill in such a way as to have a tremendous impact on the action taken by the committee. The array of options that a legislative committee can undertake are as follows: (1) report a bill out favorably as is; (2) report favorably, with amendments; (3) report a substitute bill favorably; (4) report a bill out unfavorably; (5) send the bill to another committee for review; (6) table the bill, or (7) not place it on the committee's agenda.

Depending on the committee's recommendation, the next step is for the bill to go before the first house for full review. At that time, the general legislative climate should be assessed to determine whether a great amount of public support is needed.

From the first house, the bill must proceed to the second house for approval and finally to the president or governor for signature. This process clearly indicates several other key points at which intervention can take place.

THE POLITICIAN

The key component within the legislative process is the politician. As a legislator, he or she represents a large constituent group having a diversity of positions, values, and ideas that influence him or her. Politicians vary by age, experience, training, political ideology, and party affiliation. In order to understand the political process, one needs to know not only the rules and regulations, but also the players.

External to yet influential in the political process are such other factors as public opinion, media involvement, the activities of special interest groups, and informal coalitions among legislators (such as the black caucus, the liberal caucus, the senior legislators' caucus, and so forth.) Knowledge of these factors assists lobbyists in influencing legislators.

Politicians have diverse constituencies to whom they feel accountable. First, politicians are responsible to those who voted for them. Second, they have a responsibility to the population within their geographic district, last, they feel a responsibility to those individuals who campaigned for them. If politicians are listening to opposing opinions from these diverse constituent groups, decision making becomes difficult.

Another set of concerns involves limitations on the politician's time. Politicians have very little time to go out and seek problem areas and concerns that need correcting. They must rely on individuals, constituents, lobbyists, and others, to bring problems to them and to supply them with detailed information about the problems or concerns on which they are working. To further complicate matters, many state representatives have either no aides or only one aide to do research, to investigate, and to advise them. Some have access to staff members hired by the legislative body but the scope of this assistance is rather limited. Clearly, given the variety of issues that face any one legislator, often there is not enough time or staff to go around, especially when one realizes that politicians frequently are unfamiliar with many issues about which they must make decisions.

Legislators also must deal with constant public exposure. Many hours of work are allocated to understanding and dealing with conflicting views and interests. They must meet with their constituents and with special interest groups, all of whom want to advise them. As a result they may find themselves immersed in such complex social issues as abortion, euthanasia, the death penalty, and domestic violence. The advice and pressure from these groups supporting and opposing these issues often is contradictory.

Furthermore, because any individual who becomes a legislator goes through a very lengthy and costly process to get elected, a frequent concern for politicians is to maintain their position by being reelected. A candidate for the United States Congress may spend almost half of his or her term campaigning and may either avoid difficult and controversial issues during campaign years or assume a popular, noncontroversial position.

Anyone who wants to become an effective lobbyist must have a general knowledge of the factors that influence politicians' behavior. Some individuals become politicians because they want to be in the limelight and to have constant public exposure, some are deeply concerned about issues and want to make changes, and some find themselves in politics because of their family's name and prominent status. These factors may influence how a legislator perceives legislation or acts upon issues; thus lobbyists must understand them in order to have a total grasp of the politician and his or her milieu.

THE INFORMAL POLITICAL PROCESS

Lobbyists must be aware of formal legislative procedures and processes, but they also should be familiar with the informal processes. Usually viewed as "politics," the informal processes actually are individual-to-individual or group-to-group influences, motives, or relationships that affect the outcome of legislation. When attempting to influence legislation, both the formal and informal processes need to be taken into consideration.

For example, one group of legislators trying to push through a bill to create public jobs in order to decrease the unemployment rate may be opposed by another group of legislators who wish to increase a certain defense-budget item. These two groups may come together and compromise by creating defense-related jobs, thus enabling both groups to obtain their desired objectives. It is also possible, of course, for this scenario to result in the defeat of both pieces of legislation.

In addition to caucuses or groupings of legislators by state, by party affiliation, and by issue, other influences exist that can have an informal effect upon legislation. First, the piece of legislation in which you are interested may not have as high a priority in the eye of the public as does other legislation. Second, because legislators may have so many other items to deal with, your piece of legislation may be dealt with only superficially in order to appease you. Finally, legislation will be dealt with by the politician in respect to its possible impact on his or her career and reelection.

LOBBYING

Goal Setting   Once a lobbyist understands the formal and informal process a bill must go through and has a grasp of the players (politicians, aides, other lobbyists), the next step is to formulate a clearly defined goal. One must decide whether to influence already-proposed pieces of legislation, modify present legislation, or develop a new piece of legislation. To enlist others in a lobbying effort, an explicit goal is essential. Whatever the goal, it should be stated clearly, and, ideally, in measurable terms so that it will be possible to know if it has been achieved.

Strategy Setting   Setting strategy is a critical and often neglected part of lobbying. Without it lobbying may be ineffectual. *Strategy* is the plan of action for the achievement of the goal. As soon as the goal has been identified and operationalized, the strategy should be determined.

A parallel can be drawn between strategy setting and management by objectives, where the goal is defined and the various steps to reach that goal are stated. It is clear to all participants what steps are needed in order to proceed to the goal. In the delineation of strategy, any complicating factors or unforeseen obstacles that may delay or block action should be spelled out, and alternative strategies should be developed in case complicating factors or obstacles arise.

For example, legislation is introduced at the state level to restore allocation levels for primary and secondary public education. Passage appears likely, despite the state's fiscally constrained condition, because it is difficult to oppose education for young children. However, the state is plagued by high rates of unemployment, and several mayors have requested the governor to proclaim a state of emergency because of the decreasing nutritional level of a large segment of the state's population who are unable to afford adequate amounts of food. This crisis could overshadow concern for public education.

It is impossible to describe all alternative strategies that could be adopted. A strategy must be developed after a review of the policy and the politicians involved, an assessment of the bill's likely trail, an understanding of potential legislative and community climates, and an assessment of what possibilities are realistic for the lobbyists.

One strategy may be to systematically work with and educate key legislators as the legislation is developed, amended, and passed through committees; that is, a strategy for working within the legislative system to overcome resistance and to educate. An alternative and potentially conflict-producing strategy at the opposite end of the continuum is to amass public support and encourage numerous contacts with legislators (Ornstein & Elder, 1978).

Usually it is desirable to first attempt to work within the system and then, when and if opposition develops, to move to an external strategy. A middle approach might be used in a situation in which a piece of legislation appears to have majority support but faces a potential floor debate. In such a case, a letter campaign to the general assembly or the presence of concerned citizens during a legislative session may prove effective.

A social worker/lobbyist should keep in mind several essential concepts. First, it is important to be honest and factual whenever a legislator or legislative aide is contacted. Second, and perhaps more important, it is well to remember that straightforward presentations with data generally provide the most persuasive approach and maintain the credibility of both the social worker/lobbyist and the social work profession. Finally, any presentation should include answers to two questions of critical concern to legislators: (1) What will this proposed legislation cost? (2) What is the social impact of this bill? It is particularly important to anticipate not only the answers to these questions, but, if the costs appear high, to provide information about the costs of allowing the social problem or need to go unresolved.

At the beginning of any lobbying effort, the lobbyist must keep in mind that a variety of checks and balances are built into the legislative process, and that legislators can be influenced in numerous ways. The process is complex, with formal as well as informal variables; hundreds of concerns and points of view are concurrently presented before any legislative body. Thus, a lobbyist must have two important qualities: patience and persistence.

In conclusion, the lobbyist should bear in mind the following guidelines:

1. Know your issue thoroughly. Anticipate the opposition's claims and formulate persuasive counterarguments. Be prepared to provide technical information that will be useful to the politician(s) involved.
2. Identify a core group of committed and effective workers who will lead a coalition of interested groups and individuals who can be called on to write letters, lobby, or publicize the issue.
3. Locate a lawmaker who is sympathetic to your issue and is likely to be effective in advancing the cause and continue to work with him or her for the duration of the process.
4. Be familiar with the formal legislative structure and the procedural steps a bill must take to become a law.
5. Spend as much time as possible at the capitol, both to answer legislators' questions and to be in a position to intervene effectively at the critical moment, by offering advice or information before decisions have been made. (Michigan Sea Grant Advisory Service, 1981).

In addition to patience and persistence, another extremely important attribute of a lobbyist is the ability to acknowledge the merits of competing proposals. Although a lobbyist's role is to mobilize the strongest and most persuasive arguments for his or her position, when a lobbyist becomes unable or unwilling to acknowledge the merits of an alternative proposal, he or she is seen as a propagandist, and his or her credibility and eventual utility may be dismissed (Patti & Dear, 1981.)

COALITION BUILDING

Experience has shown that the larger the group of individuals who want a piece of legislation passed, the greater the possibility of passage. Because there is strength in numbers, a lobbyist should include coalition building as part of his or her total strategy.

A *coalition* is a loosely woven, ad hoc association of constituent groups, each of whose primary identification is outside the coalition (Humphreys, 1979). Social workers engaged in coalition building usually seek linkages with those who are most sympathetic to their ideas, values, and, philosophies, such as mental health associations, children's defense funds, and so forth, but all too often, social workers overlook potential alliances with groups that may appear on the surface unlikely to be supportive of social work policies. It is important that all aspects of a given issue be carefully examined to identify points of potential commonality. For example, in 1983, when Congress was considering an increase in the gasoline tax to generate revenues for the improvement of roads and bridges, this effort was supported by human service professionals because it would create jobs for the unemployed. Although this was the central issue that garnered the support of human service professionals, road builders and construction workers also supported the legislation, forming an otherwise unlikely coalition of the two groups.

The more diversified the groups in the coalition, the more powerful the coalition becomes. At the same time, however, the greater the diversity, the more vulnerable the coalition is to being splintered by outside opposing groups. When an organization or coalition is splintered at a critical moment, it can lose support for the legislation, because without unanimous support from the coalition, legislators may not even bother to discuss the legislation with representatives of the group (Mahaffey, 1972).

FACE-TO-FACE LOBBYING

Social workers who are naive about politicians and the political process may believe that politicians are so powerful that they are unapproachable. It seems easier to them to write letters, sign petitions, or join coalitions than to interact directly with legislators. Nonetheless, legislators need direct interaction and may, in fact, even seek it out from various individuals and groups, because usually they realize that they are very much isolated and protected from what is really occurring in society, and therefore must rely on input from credible sources.

In face-to-face lobbying with a legislator whom the lobbyist has never met, one must establish credibility by identifying who he or she is representing as well as his or her personal expertise and experience. Particularly if one is a constituent of that legislator, a basis for rapport may already exist. Having been visibly active in a legislator's campaign is certainly beneficial in establishing a relationship, because campaigns are expensive and politicians generally dislike fundraising, so they are likely to remember those who assisted and supported them in that process (Mahaffey, 1972).

It is unnecessary to buy a legislator a three-martini lunch. Straightforward, factual, and well-presented information is most effective. Although legislative offices and surroundings might be intimidating to the beginning lobbyist, remember that the representative needs your information and assistance. Legislators are extremely busy and often must deal with a multitude of subject areas. Thus, they might switch subjects during an interview. Also, they sometimes deliberately take a contrary stance, but this may be because they want to learn how to argue effectively on behalf of your position.

Developing a good working relationship with a legislator's secretary should not be overlooked. Often secretaries are gatekeepers. As such, they represent a potential access point to the legislator and a channel through which information can be transmitted that may influence the legislator.

Many lobbyists focus their efforts on legislators who share values and goals similar to their own. Although such legislators are valuable, they may not be the most important target of influence (Patti & Dear, 1981). When deciding whom to contact, several lists should be compiled—one consisting of legislators overtly supportive of your position, another of those who are explicitly opposed, and a third composed of those who are undecided. The third list is the one that should be targeted for intensive effort. At the same time, keep in contact with supporters through informative letters, phone calls, and the like.

Before a face-to-face interview with a representative, preparation is in order. Determine what particular issues are of interest, how he or she approaches certain subjects, and what position he or she has taken on similar legislation in the past. This will allow you to present material in a way that encourages the legislator to listen to your position. Present the information to the legislator, keeping in mind the importance (to him or her) of the cost of the proposal and its social implications.

Almost all legislators will grant an appointment on request. However, in dealing with members of Congress, particularly if one is attempting to see them in Washington, time constraints may require that the appointment be with a legislative aide. Do not be dismayed. In most cases, the aides are the ones who formulate policy and persuade the legislator to take a position. When possible, ask for an appointment in the legislator's home district, where committee pressures and other responsibilities are somewhat reduced. Remember that the legislator is in his or her home district to get constituents' opinions on issues.

Because the length of appointments is likely to be limited, it is an excellent idea to provide written material and supportive documentation. Be sure that this material is as succinct as possible. A copy of all written material also should be provided for the legislative aide. Remember that it is important to utilize case examples from the legislator's district whenever possible.

Obtaining an appointment with state and local officials is usually easier, and these meetings often occur in less formal settings, such as political gatherings, receptions, and in the corridors of the statehouse or county building. However, do not invade the politician's personal life by accosting him or her at the grocery store or theater. In all settings, common courtesy should be used, and, regardless of the outcome of the discussion, thank the legislator for his or her time and open-mindedness. Follow up the meeting with a thank you letter that includes a synopsis of the position taken by the legislator during that meeting. Finally, follow through with anything that you agreed to do. If you fail to do so, your credibility will quickly deteriorate.

LETTER WRITING

It is commonly believed that letters to legislators are never read. This is a myth. The fact is that they are read most carefully, particularly if they come from constituents. Letters indicate that constituents are sufficiently concerned about an issue to take the time to write.

Letters to legislators should be short, to the point, and credible. They should describe exactly what your position is and, if necessary, provide documentation. Avoid form letters, postcards, and telegrams. These are viewed as efforts by groups and not as opinions of individuals.

Never threaten a legislator. This will be counterproductive and will cause you to lose your credibility and to be discarded as an "angry individual." The legislator should be thanked for considering your views and, if you are comfortable with such a statement, for the hard work the legislator has undertaken on other issues of concern. A short thank you after any vote on a piece of legislation with which you agree will testify to the depth of your interest and may enhance your credibility when other issues arise.

TESTIFYING

A legislative committee struggling to understand the intracacies of a complicated piece of legislation will solicit testimony as a means to gather as much information as possible on various aspects of the legislation in the shortest amount of time. Indeed, if the legislators had endless hours to sit and talk with a variety of individuals, testimony would be much less useful, but because time is limited, testimony offers an excellent opportunity for the general public to have input into a committee's decision. Testimonial sessions often are conducted in various parts of the state or nation, to ensure access to more people and to a diversity of points of views (Sharwell, 1982).

In the testimonial process the committee listens to statements about the legislation and to information helpful to their decision making. The legislators also can ask questions of the person testifying, and any legislator can request particular individuals to appear before the committee or subcommittee to testify. Testifying is an ideal opportunity for the media to gather public opinion, and for individuals to have a tremendous amount of input into legislative decisions. The following are some reasons why written testimony should be provided:

It demonstrates professionalism.

It shows a more than casual interest in the legislative matter.

It ensures that the committee record of the testimony will be accurate.

It can make the oral presentation to the committee more effective, because some of the committee members and the committee staff will read the written statement in addition to listening to the testimony.

It permits the advocate to say all he or she wants to say in the written statement while still being able to meet the time restraints often imposed by oral testimony.

It provides flexibility in that the advocate can cover all the issues in the written statement but can highlight points in the oral portion that are particularly responsive to points by opponents.

It provides greater assurance that media coverage of the testimony will be fuller and more accurate, because media representatives can work from the written statement rather than from hastily penciled notes.

It enables the advocate to inform members of the organization represented and other persons and organizations about the content of the testimony.

It provides a better record for the advocate's own organization than will notes from memory. (Sharwell, 1982)

Copies of written testimony should be provided to committee members, aides, and the media.

In addition to written testimony, have a summary ready to read aloud. Read slowly, and clearly and take any interruptions calmly. When asked a question or for clarification, answer in a straightforward manner. If you do not have an answer, defer by saying that you would like to answer in writing.

The key to effective legislative lobbying is preparation. This is especially true when testifying. Although preparation takes a considerable amount of time, it is necessary to increase one's chances of success.

CONCLUSION

Lobbying efforts have a reputation for being manipulative and self-serving. However, the reality of the American political system indicates that these efforts have become necessary to successful influencing of the legislative process.

The social work profession needs to become more astute in the practices and skills involved in lobbying. The various facets of the political process—legislative and committee rules and regulations and formal and informal decision-making processes—have created a milieu that social work professionals have avoided. Lobbying for human service legislation is not self-serving, but, rather, is consistent with client advocacy.

If more social workers were to acquire the techniques outlined in this chapter, the authors are confident that more humane social policies would be developed and enacted. Lobbying is indeed an essential interventive strategy in social work.

This chapter has only touched on the various aspects of lobbying techniques. It is a primer for social workers who wish to advocate for human service goals. The skill with which social workers participate in the political system is an important factor in determining their influence on the formation of social policy. Immense resources neither are required nor will guarantee social workers a significant influence in the political arena. Rather, the success of the profession's endeavors will be determined by social workers' ability to utilize both effective lobbying skills and their unique mix of professional skills.

ASSIGNMENTS

1. Learn how a bill becomes a law in your state.
2. Determine when a testimonial hearing for a bill you are interested in will occur. Develop a position statement and then testify at that hearing.
3. Develop a position on a current legislative issue, and make an appointment with your own state legislator to influence his or her vote.

SUGGESTED READINGS

Patti, Rino, and Ronald Dear. "Legislative Advocacy: Seven Effective Tactics." *Social Work*, 26 (July 1981): pp. 289–296.

Mahaffey, Maryann. "Lobbying and Social Work." *Social Work*, 17 (January 1972): pp. 3–11.

REFERENCES

Humphreys, Nancy. "Competing for Revenue Sharing Funds: A Coalition Approach." *Social Work*, 24 (January 1979): pp. 14–18.

Mahaffey, Maryann, "Lobbying and Social Work." *Social Work*, 17 (January 1972): pp. 3–11.

Mahaffey, Maryann, and John Hanks (Eds.), *Practical Politics*. Washington, DC: National Association of Social Workers, 1982.

Michigan Sea Grant Advisory Service. *How Citizens Can Influence Legislation in Michigan*. Lansing: Michigan State University Cooperative Extension Service, 1981.

Ornstein, Norman, and Elder Shirley. *Interest Groups, Lobbying and Policy Making.* Washington, DC: Congressional Quarterly Press, 1978.

Patti, Rino, and Ronald Dear. "Legislative Advocacy: Seven Effective Tactics." *Social Work*, 26 (July 1981): pp. 289–296.

Sharwell, George. "How to Testify Before a Legislative Committee." In Mahaffey, Maryann and John Hanks (Eds.), *Practical Politics*. (Washington, DC: National Association of Social Workers, 1982): pp. 85–99.

7
Monitoring the Bureaucracy

After months of hard work, a social worker who had been lobbying for passage of a bill was informed that the state senate had passed the bill and the governor had signed it. Much effort had resulted in legislative victory. Or had it?

On the contrary, social workers all too often win the legislative battle and proceed to lose the war by assuming their work is finished (Curren, 1982). Legislatures must not only pass bills but fund them, and if they do not fund a bill after passage (as sometimes occurs), that bill effectively is killed. Nor is funding the last of the hurdles. Administrative rules may be written that misinterpret the legislators' intent, or agencies may implement the regulations in a manner that differs from the intent.

The purpose of monitoring the bureaucracy is to assure that the intent of the legislation is carried out. The social work lobbyist needs to monitor four areas after a bill has been passed: (1) promulgation of rules; (2) implementation and adherence to the rules by agencies; (3) executive orders and administrative changes; and (4) the budget allocation process.

Monitoring should not be confused with lobbying. Monitoring is the process of keeping a watchful eye on the government to see that the legislative intent is carried out, whereas lobbying is the act of influencing legislation. Monitoring and lobbying have some elements in common yet are distinctly different activities. For example, a social worker who discovers an inconsistency between the intent of the law and its subsequent implementation might use the lobbying techniques described in Chapter 6 to rectify the situation. The greatest overlap between the two activities occurs when the administrative rules are being promulgated for a recently passed piece of legislation. During this period, a certain amount of lobbying as well as monitoring may take place. In either case, the social worker must develop an interventive strategy, deciding how most effectively to induce others to modify their policy in the desired direction (Dluhy, 1982).

Throughout this chapter, we refer to the "intent" of legislation, by which we mean the ultimate goal the supporters of the original bill had in mind. Throughout the entire legislative process, from the initial drafting of a bill to its funding and implementation, various interpretations, modifications and deliberate misconstruals can result in a program whose characteristics are inconsistent with the original intent of a bill. Consider tax bills, where Congress attempts to stimulate certain business or economic activities through tax breaks, but finds that because of regulatory loopholes or misinterpretations, not only have government revenues been reduced but other unintended tax breaks also have been created.

It is important for the social worker to understand that certain formal and informal steps related to policy adoption and implementation apply to all levels of government: (1) rule writing and promulgation, (2) rule implementation, and (3) budget allocation. In addition, one must be aware of the importance of executive orders and other administrative changes that subsequently may affect program implementation.

Rule writing and promulgation occurs shortly after the bill is signed by the president, governor, or mayor. The promulgation processes usually occur just once, although legislation may be amended, repealed, or replaced at any time, after which the promulgation and implementation process will recur. Administrative orders, agency compliance, and the budget allocation process require more continuous or at least repeated scrutiny. In addition, even after a law has been enacted, a continuous surveillance of the program and the budgetary process is necessary to assure that the services and benefits that were the intended result of the law are being provided.

The intent of this chapter is to inform the reader about the complex processes that occur after a bill is passed and the effect these can have. Monitoring skills are essential in the repertoire of political interventions. We will provide strategies for effective monitoring in the three areas listed previously and will indicate how social work skills can be utilized in the monitoring process.

PROMULGATING THE RULES

A law is a mandate from the legislative body that provides guidelines to govern behavior and decision making; administrative regulations provide directives for the law's implementation. With a few exceptions, the promulgation of rules is similar to the process by which a bill becomes a law. Instead of a legislative committee, however, the administrative branch is responsible for the design and development of rules (see Table 7.1).

The purpose of rules is to inform both the general public and those who

TABLE 7.1 Comparison of the Steps in Rule Writing and in Drafting a Bill

Rule writing	Drafting a bill
1. Public hearings	1. Public hearings
2. Approval of department	2. Approval of department
3. Committee approval	3. Committee approval
4. Approval of house and senate	4. Approval of house and senate
5. Governor's approval	5. Governor's approval

administer the legislation how the law will be implemented and enforced. Regulations may be perceived as policy statements that transform the legislative ideal into practical design and delivery stages. Regulations usually sharpen and clarify staffing requirements, service-provider responsibilities, client eligibility, treatment modalities, and accountability and reporting mechanisms. These regulations are not merely simplistic extensions of the legislation. Indeed, the rule-making process provides an opportunity to make decisions about the basic allocation of services that can considerably alter the original intent of the legislation.

Usually there is no time limit on writing a set of rules satisfactory to all concerned with a particular law. A delay in rule writing may be a means to weaken or skew the law's intent. Public input usually is sought during the rule-writing stage, either in written form addressed to the administrative staff engaged in rule writing, or at public hearings scheduled by the agency. The substance and political importance of public input is weighed by the agency prior to issuing the final regulations (Pierce, 1984). It is possible for the executive (the president or governor) to implement emergency rules while awaiting the final draft from the appropriate agency. This too can have long-term effects.

Although there are many similarities between the processes of bill passage and rule writing, there are differences also. Additional steps may be involved in either process, and these can vary from state to state or among city and county governments. Procedures described in Chapter 6 on lobbying must be used during all of the steps involved in the promulgation of the rules.

The first decision made in the rule-writing phase is to decide which agency will be assigned the task. Unless otherwise specified within the bill, the chief elected official (the president or governor) makes this decision. Once delegated to a specific division of an agency, agency personnel are assigned to complete the task. In general, any rule-writing assignment is in addition to the other job responsibilities of the personnel involved. The end product will, of course, reflect the values, knowledge (or lack thereof), expertise, and concern of these staff members.

After a draft set of rules has been developed, public input is sought. In most states the rules and regulations must be approved by state legal authorities, such as the attorney general's office, and a joint rules committee of both legislative houses, which can (1) decide not to adopt the rules and send them back for further clarification, (2) pass them as presented, or (3) take no action. Finally, the entire legislative body must approve the rules by a majority vote. The rules and regulations then are returned to the president or governor for final approval.

Now the rules and regulations can be implemented. However, once implementation begins and even after services have been begun to be offered, the legislature can change the regulations via a resolution, passage of an amended bill, or budgetary allocation. Any of these processes can substantially modify the intent of the initial bill (Curren, 1982).

Within the rule-writing process, many stages may require monitoring and intervention. A logical starting point is with the staff member assigned to write the regulations. An excellent approach at this stage is to set up an appointment with the staff member to provide brief and factual input. A straightforward demonstration of interest in the process and willingness to assist could be of great importance, because the staff member involved may have limited knowledge and expertise on the subject of the rules and limited time to complete the task (Curren, 1982). If possible, it is useful to not only think through but to write out a proposal prior to such a meeting. Staff members may willingly borrow from your ideas. At a minimum, they almost certainly will give them consideration, because most states require consideration and evaluation of any input given to those who are writing or promulgating rules.

Providing input at public hearings is another opportunity to influence the direction of administrative regulations. It is essential to keep track of times, dates, and locations of public hearings to assure that your representatives are present. As with testimony during the lobbying process, written statements should be provided as well, given the time limitations on verbal presentations.

Finally, it is important to provide input to legislators prior to the final adoption of the regulations. Consider, for example, a law to establish an inner-city drug-treatment program. The regulations for such a program should specify the type and qualifications of administrators, therapists, and support staff and should establish the targeted clients, eligibility standards, fee schedules, operational procedures, hours, and service parameters. All of these stipulations can dramatically affect the program. Charging a fee for treatment, for example, most assuredly would be a disincentive to poor inner-city residents and dramatically reduce the program's effectiveness. Not providing evening or weekend services would have an equally devastating effect. On the other hand, evening hours, drop-in policies, and outreach efforts might improve service delivery and increase program effectiveness.

RULE IMPLEMENTATION AND AGENCY COMPLIANCE

Once the rules have been written, their implementation must be monitored. This is best done at the beginning, when it is easier to make changes than it is after programs and procedures have become firmly established.

To be sure, there is an inherent contradiction in rules related to human services. In order to assure that the intent of the law is carried out, it may be desirable to promulgate detailed and possibly restrictive rules. Some degree of flexibility in the interpretation of those rules, however, may well allow the program to address more adequately and equitably over time a variety of individual client concerns and problems, and allow the program to respond to changing client needs as well. Loose regulations may suit the bureaucrat's interest in having administrative flexibility while easing the agency's drive for political survival (Bell & Bell, 1982). The pitfall is that this flexibility also may allow services to change as popular opinions dictate, regardless of recipient needs.

The issues involved in specifying staff qualifications for a particular human service program offer a useful illustration of this type of dilemma. For example, a rigid requirement that only MSWs with mental health training will be acceptable as therapists in a drug-treatment program when applied statewide, may represent an unfairly restrictive qualification, if such personnel are not available in all areas of the state. However, the often-used alternative of establishing "minimum qualifications," (e.g., a minimum requirement of a high school diploma or 12 credit hours of human service training) may result in untrained staff providing direct services and even therapy to program clients.

Monitoring rule implementation is necessary not only to protect the general public's rights, but also to assure agency adherence to the regulations. Some of the major reasons why implementation may deviate from legislative intent are as follows:

1.   All agencies, including human service agencies, have vested interests to protect—not only their budgets but also their organizational structure and general service-delivery design. After an organization is established, any modification, whether it be expansion, contraction, or extinction, will create a great deal of resistance. When states enacted child abuse legislation in the late 1970s, strong resistance arose when the responsibility for investigation and reporting was assigned to state public welfare departments or child welfare agencies that already were overburdened.

2.   Social agencies, despite the lofty language in their charters and in social legislation, are not necessarily benign with respect to protecting clients' rights. Once reimbursement for the services have been exhausted, the client all too often is disregarded or referred to another agency. When the Title XX

amendments to the Social Security Act mandated that 50 percent of all funded services be delivered to current welfare recipients, several states initiated "head hunts" to increase welfare rolls so that they would have more clients to serve.

3. Legitimate differences in interpreting legislative intent can occur. For example, the use of flexible terminology in listing requirements, such as "social work degree or the equivalent," could be interpreted to mean "MSW" but also legitimately could be taken to mean "MSW or MA in psychology or sociology," or even "B.A. with life or professional experience equivalents."

4. State and federal budgetary-oversight agencies have veto power over state agencies when it comes to administrative decisions made in the course of implementing social legislation, and this power is sometimes exercised to the detriment of groups of clients who were intended to benefit from the legislation. For example, mothers on the Aid to Families with Dependent Children program often are directed by agencies to find work, when in fact the intent of the law that established the program was to encourage mothers to stay home and raise their children. In such cases, budgetary agencies need to be challenged on their interpretation of legislative intent (Bell & Bell, 1982).

5. Public pressure caused by a misunderstanding of a program might cause legislators, administrators, and agency staff to make changes that ultimately alter the intent and effectiveness of the program. For example, encouraging AFDC mothers to find work, without also providing adequate day care, will result in less adequate care for the children involved than was the case before the program was enacted.

6. The covert purpose of the law differs from the public justification for it, thus complicating the measurement of its effectiveness. For instance, many job-training programs for the poor were enacted not to assist people to become economically self-sufficient, but rather to stimulate the economy or reduce welfare rolls.

In sum, agencies may deliberately or mistakenly misinterpret administrative regulations, which can result in deviation from legislative intent at the point of program initiation. Social workers within and without the organizations that administer such programs must monitor and intervene at this stage to assure consistency with legislative intent. A number of monitoring operations may be legislatively mandated, such as administrative auditing, program review and evaluation, or compliance with quality-control measures. Also, state "sunset laws" may require external review of the agency. Getting appointed to an advisory committee with oversight functions is one important and powerful method of monitoring these necessary internal or external review processes.

Budget Allocations The budget is the clearest and most measurable indicator of governmental priorities. It lies at the heart of the political process and requires a great deal of continuous monitoring (Wildavsky, 1979). Legislators have the opportunity either annually or biannually, to enhance or undermine the effectiveness of a program or agency via budget allocations. A good example of this occurred during President Reagan's first term of office. The Health Systems Act had received a $1.25 per capita allocation in 1980 but was cut to .38 cents per capita two years later, leaving the agency unable to meet the goals originally established in the legislation.

The size and design of a budget is a matter of serious contention in our political life (Wildavsky, 1979). The budget not only proposes what is to be expended, but projects revenues as well. The federal budget which can have a deficit, follows an atypical budgetary process, because most state, local, and private budgets must be balanced or show a reserve. On the state and local levels, overly optimistic revenue projections by a governor or mayor may cause the administrative branch to react by reducing expenditures in order to maintain a balanced budget. Thus, revenue projections are just as important as proposed expenditures.

Just as flexibility in interpretation of legislation can have both positive and negative consequences, flexibility in how budgets are presented also can have contradictory effects. Budgets may be presented and approved as lump sums for entire state administrative units, by line items, or by departmental functions. If budgetary oversight, approval, and allocation is by line item or by departmental function legislators can provide more direction and input over agency priorities. A lump-sum budget-appropriation process, however, may allow for too much latitude and administrative discretion by the agency chief executive.

The budget-allocation process can be influenced in several ways. One is to influence the type of budget that will be presented and approved. If social workers want extreme latitude, they should lobby for lump-sum budgets. Second, because department heads make funding recommendations to the budget director, the strategy used by the department head can be crucial. For example, if a department head requests an extremely large increase after several years of small, incremental budget increases, this will create legislative interest. If the need for the request is well documented and publicly supported, it may be granted. On the other hand, it is likely that undocumented requests for large budget increases will be disregarded.

As mentioned earlier, budget allocations have a great impact upon policy implementation. For that reason, monitoring the budgetary process is highly important, even crucial, to program maintenance and service delivery. Social workers have both firsthand experience and aggregate data from previous budget cycles on the impact of differing funding levels on client service. This information should be supplied to the legislative budget office before a new budget is proposed. Presented regularly, such information can be used to sensitize fiscal planners to the impact of funding levels on client service and to projections of future demand. After the budget is proposed, the next logical intervention is lobbying the legislature, because after the budget is amended and approved by the legislative branch, it is returned to the administrative branch for signature and implementation, and further intervention becomes difficult.

The most obvious and yet most controversial issue in budget allocations for human services is to define and operationalize "adequate standards and services." *Operationalization* refers to staff size, staff qualifications, caseload ratios, and hours of service delivery. A common value dilemma social work program staff face is how to deliver quality services to all needy clients when funds are limited or decreasing funds, without turning clients away. Although in the short-term it is not in the best interest of the client to be denied service, waiting-list figures indicating unmet needs can be powerful indicators to legislators of the need for increased funding for expanding a particular service.

Administrative Changes or Executive Orders
Once a bill has been enacted, responsibility for the programs it creates rests with the chief executive officer or the department head, who often is empowered to make certain administrative changes. If any changes in the rules are then made, the same process mentioned earlier will be followed. However, there are ways in which administrators can affect a program without changing the rules. One is to recommend a reduced budget.

Another subtle mechanism for circumventing legislative intent is to exercise power over the way responsibilities for the program are assigned. To take an extreme example, assigning program responsibilities to one agency, or to one agency staff member, may signal limited interest in effective program implementation. Likewise, assigning responsibility for the program to an inappropriate agency could predetermine its failure. Therefore, monitoring such administrative actions is a critical interventive task.

Nonenforcement of the rules through administrative oversight is another way to undermine the intent of a piece of legislation. If the law does not include evaluative or accountability requirements or procedures, noncompliance is likely. For example, the Hill–Burton Act required hospitals to provide a percentage of their health care service free to the poor in exchange for federal loans. Under the act, participating hospitals were required to inform poor patients of the availability of the free services. However, because no agency was designated to oversee the hospitals on this point, many hospitals did not comply with the regulation.

Other unobtrusive methods can be used by an executive to alter the outcome of a program: placing a freeze on staff replacements; overloading a specific agency subdivision; rewarding noncompliance; changing eligibility requirements; reducing publicity and outreach. All of these methods will alter the amount and pattern of services provided.

SOCIAL WORK SKILLS

All of the rule-making and rule-implementing processes mentioned in this chapter require consistent monitoring in order to assure that the intent of the law is carried out and that the clients targeted by the legislation receive mandated services. Because elected officials, agency staff, public opinion, and society's needs change, social workers must monitor from both outside and inside the bureaucracy. They also need to utilize social work skills to ensure that program goals and services remain appropriate. Although this type of ongoing monitoring is difficult and tedious, it is nevertheless essential and is quite compatible with social work skills as well. The same basic problem-solving approach that social workers use with clients can be employed in monitoring a program: identify the problem; gather information; make an assessment; develop a plan of action.

Problem identification may seem to be the most straightforward of the stages, because usually it is evident that clients have unmet needs or are falling between service areas. What may not be evident is in which of the stages the fault lies—legislative enactment, program design and delivery, or budget allocation. Once this has been determined, appropriate information can be collected and presented.

Information is the key to effective advocacy. Persuasive information comes in many forms. Quantitative data may be collected and presented, such as the percentage of the population in need, the number of clients served, or the number of population "at risk." Information may be presented comparatively, in the form of data specifying proportions of the population in need or ratios of clients served county-to-county or state-to-state. The same information also can be collected and presented in qualitative terms, by citing case illustrations, or by projecting additional problems or future scenarios if the current need is not met.

Regardless of type, information gathered by social workers can increase their ability to influence public officials. Facts collected about community problems will generate good questions, identify hidden problems, and support or challenge government policies and explanations. Information also lends credibility to opinions. It also enables one to reveal officials' evasions, question their assumptions, and, if necessary, expose errors or inconsistencies in their figures (Shur & Smith, 1980).

Data can be found in a number of places. The census is a useful resource and much of the data in it is already crosstabulated, enhancing its utility. For example, one can easily retrieve data on income levels by sex, household size, or occupational status of household head. Guides to the census include the *Directory of Federal Statistics for Local Areas: A Guide to Sources* (U.S. Bureau of the Census, 1978), which provides a complete subject and geographical index of most statistics collected by the federal government, and the *Census Users Guide*, (U.S. Bureau of the Census, 1980), a more technical book that includes definitions of all terms used in the census.

Another type of information that may be useful for advocacy in the monitoring stages covers program rules, regulations, and procedures is the *Catalog of Federal Domestic Assistance* (U.S. General Services Administration), which contains a complete description of federal programs, including eligibility criteria, application timing and procedures, citations to controlling laws and regulations, and funding available. A publication called *Geographic Distribution of Federal Funds* (U.S. Community Services Administration) identifies most of the federally funded programs in communities, including those run by private organizations. Many federal programs require states to submit state plans, which may provide data on many areas of interest. Federal law requires that copies of state plans be made available to the public through the governor's office.

Various other sources of data exist: Every two years, the Department of Health and Human Services conducts a national survey of AFDC participants and programs. States must prepare public assistance manuals that describe their rules and procedures for administering AFDC programs. The United States Government Printing Office (GPO) publishes almost 300 subject bibliographies. The Washington Information Directory lists organizations working on federal and even state-level legislation and programs. Clearly, much of this information is invaluable. However, because increasingly fewer reporting requirements are being enacted, this kind of data collection may no longer be mandated, so much data of this type will no longer be available to the public (Shur & Smith, 1980).

Whenever secondary sources of data are utilized, the inherent biases in the collection, collation, and analysis must be taken into account. Particularly when using state agency plans and reports, be aware that the need to justify a program may bias the presentation of information. Using census data, government reports, and state plans, both a projection of needs and an assessment of output and outcome can be obtained for the purpose of defending the existence or expansion of any program or service. After the information is collected and tabulated, the position must be presented in a style and format that is persuasive to those responsible for decision making. For example, stating that .003 percent of all children in a particular county were sexually molested last year may be accurate, but is less effective than dramatizing it. You can make this point more effectively by stating that for each member of the six-person committee, 100 children were unwillingly forced into sexual acts by an adult. The general problem is to decide when statistics are useful, which statistics will be most persuasive, and when a more dramatic and personal approach will be more effective.

The final stage in the monitoring process is to develop a plan of action not only for the presentation of information, but also for ongoing monitoring and lobbying to ensure that a particular position is carried through.

A word of caution is in order here: Rhetorical excess and incorrect or purposeful misuse of factual data can discredit even the best of lobbyists. Trite phrases can divert attention from the issues. Although personalizing statistics may be a persuasive tactic, sensationalizing them could be detrimental to your cause.

An illustration of monitoring agency compliance with administrative regulations can be drawn from the previously mentioned Hill–Burton Act. With the recent emergence of the "new poor," the need for federally funded health services has greatly increased. One regulation created by the act is that hospitals must post a sign in their emergency rooms and waiting areas stating that they are Hill–Burton hospitals and that services are available without cost to those without funds. However, many hospitals did not comply with this regulation. It was only through monitoring of hospitals and the threat of a law suit by a group of social workers that hospitals were forced to follow through with their obligation to advertise and provide these services to the poor.

A similar example involves a social worker who monitored a state commission that oversaw the implementation of the state's bloc grants. This person diligently attended every commission meeting to ensure that the commission was complying with the original intent of the legislators. She became so skilled at monitoring individual commissioner members that she could predict their decisions and individual preferences by their posture, facial expressions, and gestures, and subsequently could alter her interventive style or content. What is not said often can be a clue, as can body posture, gestures, and word usage. Awareness of the external factors affecting committee members or chairpersons can be important in determining the most appropriate interventive strategy. The ability to observe and understand group processes, formal and informal leadership, and committee members' personal goals and ambitions are all essential in effective intervention.

It should be obvious at this point that individuals, either alone or as part of a decision-making body, are the primary actors in all of the monitoring processes discussed in this chapter—from legislative enactment to rule writing to agency compliance. Social work skills and social workers' experience are tremendous assets in the monitoring stages.

CONCLUSION

Monitoring is the process of overseeing that rules and regulations, budget allocations, and agency compliance are consistent with the intent of the law. Social work skills are very effective in all stages of this process.

Monitoring all of these stages takes time and a great deal of patience, and is probably the most boring of the political interventive techniques, yet it is a necessary step to assure that the original intent of a piece of legislation is indeed implemented. The effect that an individual can have on the outcome may be even greater than during the initial legislative process. This is not to say that lobbying for the passage of a bill is not necessary, but that many mistakenly think that once a bill is signed, no further advocacy is necessary.

ASSIGNMENTS

1. Choose a recently enacted piece of state legislation and follow it to the agency assigned to write the rules. Obtain a copy of the administrative regulations and assess how closely they appear to follow the intent of the legislation.
2. Identify individuals or formal organizations in your state that monitor human service legislation and implementation. Describe the processes they use.

SUGGESTED READINGS

Albert, Raymond. "Social Work Advocacy in the Regulatory Process." *Social Casework*, 64 (October 1983): pp. 480–481.

Prigmore, Charles S. "Use of the Coalition in Legislative Action." *Social Work*, 19 (January 1974): pp. 96–102.

REFERENCES

Bell, William G. and Budd L. Bell. "Monitoring the Bureaucracy: An Extension of Legislative Lobbying." In Maryann Mahaffey and John W. Hanks, (Eds.), *Practical Politics: Social Work and Political Responsibility*. New York: National Association of Social Workers, 1982, pp. 118–135.

Curren, H. Patricia. Speech to the Michigan Political Action for Candidate Election Committee, October 1982.

Dluhy, Milan J. *Changing the System: Political Advocacy for Disadvantaged Groups*, Beverly Hills, CA: Sage Publications, 1982.

Pierce, Dean. *Policy for the Social Work Practitioner*. White Plains, NY: Longman, 1984.

Shur, Janet, and Paul Smith. *Information Resources for Child Advocates*. Washington DC: Children's Defense Fund, 1980.

U.S. Bureau of the Census, Data Users Services Division. *Census of Population and Housing, 1980, Users Guide, Part A*. Washington, DC: U.S. Government Printing Office.

U.S. Bureau of the Census, Data Users Services Division. *Directory of Federal Statistics for Local Areas: A Guide to Sources, 1976.* Washington, DC: U.S. Government Printing Office, 1978.

U.S. Community Services Administration. *Geographic Distribution of Federal Funds.* Washington, DC: U.S. Government Printing Office.

U.S. General Services Administration. *Catalog of Federal Domestic Assistance.* Washington, DC: U.S. Government Printing Office.

Wildavsky, Aaron. *The Politics of the Budgetary Process.* Boston: Little Brown, 1979.

8
The Campaign

Whenever you think about a political campaign, you most likely conjure up a picture of bumper stickers, balloons, hats, rallies with impassioned speeches, and cheering crowds. But this is only a small component of what a campaign entails. This chapter provides an overview of campaigning that will encourage social workers to participate in this aspect of the political process. The purpose is not to educate the reader on how to run a campaign, nor to discuss the intricacies of campaign strategy at different governmental levels. Rather, our purpose is to reduce the fears and disillusionments that volunteers, especially social work volunteers, are likely to feel when working on a campaign.

One might ask, "Why is it necessary to become involved in a campaign?" The answer is that it is essential to elect individuals to office who will listen to the concerns of both clients and the social work profession. To have such persons in office makes the social worker's task easier when monitoring and lobbying. For a social worker to have the politician's "ear," the politician needs to know that that person put forth a certain amount of effort and time to help the him or her to obtain the office. The earlier the volunteer's support, effort, and time is put forth, the greater the return and the greater the influence on the politician. This is not to suggest that one is buying legislative votes. Presumably the reason one works on a campaign is to get into office the kind of person you want as your representative. By being involved in the beginning of the campaign, which is the most difficult stage, as well as in the later phases, one reaps the rewards that come to those who "jumped on the bandwagon" early. Also, such people are much more likely to have the candidate's ear, to be granted access when key issues are discussed, or perhaps to be offered a position, than those whose support was given later or perhaps not at all.

It must be remembered that campaigns differ depending on the level of office being sought, the intensity of the issues, and the constituencies that the candidate will represent if elected. Generally speaking, the higher the office, the more complex the campaign becomes.

The object of any political campaign is, quite simply, to win. One must be elected in order to introduce, modify, or vote for legislation. No candidate expects or needs 100 percent of the votes; to win, one must receive only a majority of all votes cast. The remainder of this chapter will explain the strategies by which this goal is met and in Chapter 9 some insights on being a candidate will be shared.

COMPONENTS OF THE CAMPAIGN

The campaign is the vehicle that initiates and communicates a consistent message to enough voters to convince a majority to vote for the candidate. Like all endeavors, planning, organization, and management are required.

Every campaign has a particular message, or theme, that communicates everything about the candidate: what he or she does; what his or her positions on the issues are; and the nature and substance of the candidate's relationships with volunteers, organizations, and constituents. Consequently, the campaign theme is much more than a slogan, although it can sometimes be captured in a slogan.

Because a candidate's theme transcends all other aspects of the campaign, it should never focus on his or her detailed positions on any one or two specific issues or pending laws, but rather, should describe the style of leadership the candidate will provide on issues in general. For example, during a deep recession a gubernatorial candidate's campaign slogan was "Jobs, Jobs, Jobs." Though it may appear that this slogan was rooted in one issue, actually it indicated that the candidate understood unemployment, the problems of the poor, economic conditions, business, the state's budget deficit—in short, everything related to earning a living, including the need for human services. The message conveyed by this slogan was one of hope, and that the candidate was the one who could restore the state to economic health.

Campaign activity, whether by the candidate, paid staff, or volunteers, is designed to convey a consistent theme to as many voters as often as possible. Communication takes place through media such as direct mail, telephone calls, posters and placards, or through personal contact.

However, a campaign must be more than a series of contacts and a hodgepodge of bumper stickers, press releases, posters, telephone calls, and mailings—no matter how frequent, consistent, or effective. Above all, a campaign must establish an emotional connection between the candidate and the electorate, a connection that actually allows people to comprehend the differences between candidates and then to choose between them by voting for one. To establish this connection, the candidate cannot rely on the communication of facts alone. Instead, he or she must reach out to and make contact with individual voters where they are, in terms of both geography and interests, and do so as persuasively as possible to gain their support on Election Day (Kleinkauf, 1982).

Ultimately, a campaign is much more than an emotional connection with voters. A campaign is also the strategic management of resources. Irrespective of its level, intensity, or field, the major resources of a campaign are time, money, and people. Because these resources are limited, they must be mobilized, developed, and stretched as far as possible to enable the campaign to contact and persuade enough voters to provide the winning margin.

The amount and utilization of each of these resources is dependent on each of the other resources as well as on external factors influencing the campaign. For example, when time is short, more people will be needed to work on the campaign, whereas tasks can be spread among fewer people when time is plentiful. Alternatively, when money is plentiful, time and people are less crucial.

No matter how abundant these resources are, all campaigns strive to increase the supply. And, finally, no campaign can survive without access to all three types of resources.

Time After the campaign has begun, time becomes limited. The election date represents a deadline that cannot be changed. Therefore, the amount of time available will greatly influence how money and people are utilized. Most election races are about five or six months long. However, the higher the office being sought, the more time the campaign will need to plan strategy, raise funds, and recruit volunteers. Presidential campaigns, for example, now tend to begin as much as four years before Election Day.

Some campaigns are relatively brief, for instance, when a legislator resigns, dies, or is impeached and a special election is held, or when a primary election occurs in a district where one party predominates. When time is available, money can be raised and volunteer activity can be extended over the full length of the campaign. The longer the time frame, the easier it is to raise funds, plan strategy, or even do with less money and people.

All too often, as Election Day approaches the working days of the campaign staff and volunteers become longer, with everyone involved working 16- to 18-hour days 7 days a week in an attempt to maximize use of the time available. Thus, in a good campaign care is taken that the staff, the volunteers, and the candidate do not become fatigued to the point of feeling disenchanted with the campaign or disconnected from the constituents.

Money Campaigns are costly. Expenses in a campaign can vary from $3000 to $5000 for a local county commissioner's race to millions of dollars for a federal senatorial or presidential race. The higher the office or the larger the district, the greater the campaign cost. In addition, if volunteers are scarce, greater financial resources will be needed to hire or purchase the services necessary to successfully execute the campaign. Cash is the one resource flexible enough to meet any need that may arise. For example, if envelopes must be addressed and the campaign has a large number of volunteers to address them, the money saved could be used on advertising, but if the number of volunteers is limited, the campaign can hire outside help and use the volunteers for a more important task, such as canvassing.

Volunteers cannot help with certain tasks, or lack the skills to do so. For example, a United States Senator cannot produce television advertising by using volunteers alone. Office space, equipment, and other such necessities cannot always be donated or loaned to a campaign. In fact, if these items are provided by supporters, they are considered campaign contributions and must be reported to the election commission.

The issues concerning campaign contributions and financial reporting were discussed in Chapter 5 on political action committees. Suffice it to say here that both federal and state statutes are quite precise as to the categorization of in-kind and cash contributions, the permissible amounts of each, and the way in which disbursements are made throughout the campaign. These statutes place ceilings on total campaign contributions and on the amount and type of contribution that can be accepted from any one source.

On numerous occasions, very wealthy individuals have literally tried to buy themselves a legislative seat by using their financial resources to purchase advertising, supporters, and so forth. Often this has been to no avail. Although finances can compensate to some extent for a lack of volunteers, it is difficult to run a successful campaign without community support.

People   Although trite, it is nevertheless true that government in the United States is of the people and by the people. There is no way in our system of government to become an elected official without the help and support of people—both constituents and volunteers.

The people who work on a campaign are crucial—not only to get the work done but also to keep up the image of the campaign. The emotional support, energy, and enthusiasm of volunteers who are also constituents often provide the best advertising possible, especially when it becomes evident that their efforts are contributing to the candidate's momentum and likelihood of success. For example, if 100 volunteers turned out to work on rally, it would be clear that many people support and believe in the candidate. The lower the level of the race, the more impressive a large turnout would be, because the support of 100 volunteers for a candidate in a county commissioner's race is much more impressive than the same turnout would be for a United States Senate race.

Each campaign needs as many constituent volunteers as possible. Efforts have been made to "carpetbag" (to suddenly move into a district and run for office) not only the candidate but the entire volunteer team. These efforts rarely succeed.

CAMPAIGN MANAGEMENT

A successful campaign not only requires time, people, and money, but needs these resources early. Therefore, it is in the potential candidate's best interest to make an early decision to run, to find endorsers, and to recruit volunteers. Lining up volunteers, money, and other support early on may deter some competitors and create a "winning attitude" for the candidate, and often will induce others to jump on the "bandwagon."

Essential to the operation of any campaign—no matter how compelling its theme or the candidate's personality—is an effective campaign plan. If the campaign theme is the message to be conveyed to voters, the campaign plan is the sequence of specific activities, all carefully budgeted, by which this message is to be conveyed.

Campaign management begins with a period of research. The necessary research includes a thorough assessment of the name recognition, physical appeal, background, and previous experience of both the prospective candidate and the opposition. It is important to know if the candidate is effective in a debate situation or in front of television cameras. For example, President Reagan is a master of the electronic media, whereas the strength of his 1984 opponent, Walter Mondale, was in person-to-person encounters.

Additional research must be done on the electorate, to determine the demographics of the district. Is it young or old, middle class or poor? Also necessary is an assessment of the political climate to determine how many candidates will be in the race, whether it will pit an experienced politician against a newcomer, if gender will be an issue, and what the voters are looking for. In lower-level races, this is done by talking with people in the community. At higher levels, comprehensive opinion polls are conducted. To offset any imbalance in time, money or people, it is necessary to review the resources likely to be available to the candidate.

Because campaigns require the performance of a variety of tasks, it is useful to recruit as many volunteers as possible with skills in interaction, finances, planning, graphic design, and other skills required to run a campaign. An accurate assessment of the volunteers' numbers, skills, and available time must be made at the outset of the campaign and these resources must be continuously monitored throughout. This allows campaign managers to make the best use of talent and time, and prevents volunteers from experiencing burnout or feeling underutilized.

Following the initial assessment, a campaign plan is developed to tie the resources to specific timed and budgeted programs that will be used to reach voters. If this is done before the campaign actually begins, usually there will be time for laying the groundwork and testing the assumptions of the campaign strategy. All of this occurs before the general public has really started to think about an election.

Campaigns seem to be a hodgepodge of activities, efforts, and loosely organized plans of action, but all successful campaigns actually are highly planned and thought out, while still appearing to be spontaneous. When a campaign appears to be off track, volunteers may become frustrated if it does not switch to a new emerging issue or challenge. Campaign strategists must continuously review shifts in the political winds as the campaign progresses. On the other hand, however, they must be very careful not to change their plans with each political shift. The result of not sticking to a strategy could be a campaign that is wishy-washy and does not address the main issue, thus failing to persuade the constituents.

In the 1984 presidential election, for example, the Democratic vice-presidential candidate, Geraldine Ferraro, was not abandoned by her party's presidential candidate, Walter Mondale, when she was strenuously interrogated by the press regarding her income taxes. Mondale's strategists advised him to take this stance because they felt that eventually the subject would be dealt with adequately and that wavering on this issue might affect the future of the campaign positions. This is not to say that a situation such as Ferraro's does not hurt a campaign. But in the long run, a sudden shift, such as selecting a new vice-presidential candidate, would have been more devastating to the campaign than public scrutiny of one aspect of Ms. Ferraro's background.

The Campaign Manager: Who Really Runs the Campaign?
Often it seems that the candidate is the one who is directing and running the campaign, because indeed it is the candidate who is seeking public office. In reality, however, the campaign is run by the campaign manager, who has an advisory committee to help determine the direction in which the campaign is and should be going. The candidate usually is a member of the committee and has input into major decisions and the general direction of the campaign, but in fact he or she has only one real function in a campaign: to meet with constituents and persuade them to vote for him or her. The management of any campaign plan requires the staffing of at least the following positions:

Campaign manager

Treasurer

Volunteer coordinator

Scheduler

Fundraiser

The demands on a candidate's time are so great that he or she cannot be bothered with the day-to-day elements of the campaign: deciding what should be written on a postcard, who should receive thank you notes, how a literature drop is to be organized and executed, and the like. But no one can persuade voters as effectively as the candidate. Thus his or her time must be spent talking to undecided voters, not managing people who already are working on the campaign (Kleinkauf, 1982).

A campaign manager is essential to every campaign, regardless of its size. The manager is the administrative officer of the campaign and will make decisions on various aspects of it. Because of the responsibilities accorded to the campaign manager, the candidate should have a long-standing relationship with him or her. Effective managerial skills are not enough.

All campaigns also must have a treasurer, someone to see that money is raised, bills are paid, and that the campaign has a solid financial plan. Many governmental reports must be filed regarding the source of contributions, the amount contributed by each, and the disbursement of campaign funds.

Higher-level campaigns have many kinds of advisors: people who assist with issues, speech writers, schedulers, and in some situations, even wardrobe consultants. In lower-level campaigns, a volunteer or staff person may serve in several capacities, such as volunteer coordinator and scheduler.

Voter Contact A candidate will have varying degrees of personal contact with voters. The ideal approach is to knock on the door of someone's home, talk to the person about the campaign, and ask for the constituent's support. To have the candidate telephone an individual and ask for his or her support is only slightly less effective. Less-effective means of contact are tactics such as sending a personal note. As in lobbying, the more effort and the more personal the touch, the more effective the pitch.

Four basic channels can be used to contact voters:

1. In-person contact by the candidate or by campaign workers
2. Telephone contact
3. Mail contact
4. Media contact

To repeat, the most effective way to solicit votes is for the candidate to meet one-on-one with individual voters. In lower-level races, more opportunities exist for individual contact with voters than during a presidential race, where it is impossible to shake hands or talk with all potential voters. However, a presidential candidate will "work the crowd," shaking as many hands as possible, because, as bizarre as it may sound, the individuals with whom they shake hands probably will be more likely to vote for the candidate than those to whom he or she presents only an issue statement. In addition, the image of personal interaction is seen by millions in newspaper pictures and on the news.

In-person contact, telephone contact, and mail contact constitute direct contact with the individual voters. As stated previously, this type of direct, systematic, and personal contact with voters is the most effective campaign technique in existence, and voters continue to be most influenced by a personal meeting with the candidate. The second most influential experience is when voters meet an enthusiastic and committed volunteer (Campaign Workbook, 1978). Least effective are media contact and, in some cases, mail pieces. These are aimed at all voters and therefore are indirect methods. No matter what method is chosen, the contact program must carry the basic campaign theme, and carry it attractively, consistently, and clearly.

Targeting   As in campaigning and lobbying, targeting is an effective and essential voter-contact strategy. In a political campaign, *targeting* means identifying those voters who can be persuaded to vote for the candidate. It is unfortunate but true that a large proportion of the people who are of age to vote are not registered to vote. Among those who are registered and will vote, three groups exist: (1) those who will vote for the candidate regardless of any campaign activity (that is, those who vote a party, ethnic, racial, or gender line); (2) those who, for these same reasons, will not vote for the candidate; and (3) those who have not made up their minds and can be persuaded one way or the other. It is toward this last group that any campaign will target its efforts.

The goal of targeting is to concentrate resources where they will be most effective. An effective campaign will not try to employ strategies equally in every precinct or with every voter. It is important to identify the precincts in which the campaign's efforts will have the greatest payoffs. The campaign staff will need to determine where the candidate has the best opportunity to persuade voters, that is, where the undecided or independent voters are concentrated.

As we have pointed out, not every vote is needed to win. A candidate needs only a majority of the votes cast. Consequently, the staff must also determine where they have the greatest potential to increase turnout among voters already committed to the candidate. Efforts to increase voter turnout consist of contacting registered voters about the election and offering such services as babysitting or transportation to and from the voting place if needed.

ISSUES

It is sometimes jokingly said by those who have been involved in political campaigns that nobody really cares about issues. Sadly, there is a great deal of truth to this statement. Even in presidential elections, small issues and one-liners can be more effective in persuading people to vote for one candidate over another than the candidate's position on the major issues of the day. The candidate's party affiliation, gender, appearance, and religious or ethnic background also can persuade a voter to support a candidate, and often are even more persuasive than a review of the candidate's stance on the issues.

The United States, given its size and its history, is made up of very diverse people. In this country, there are people from every ethnic background, every country, every conceivable occupation, belief, and culture. Although this diversity poses fewer problems in lower-level races, it still has some effect on election outcomes. In order to obtain the required 51 percent of the votes, candidates attempt to take a neutral stance on as many issues as their ethics allow. On the issue of abortion, for example, some candidates have stated that they are personally against abortion but would allow a woman the right to determine what is done to her body.

Although it is also true that political action committees and special interest groups will want to know how a candidate stands on certain issues and will base their support or opposition upon this information, both the public and campaign volunteers become very frustrated with a candidate who takes a hard stance on certain issues, because this can be as devastating to the campaign as refusing to take any position at all. Also, if a candidate takes one position when talking to one group and a totally opposite one when meeting with another, this can backfire and be more damaging than if the candidate had taken a tough stance or no stance at all.

Because candidates tend to avoid taking positions, especially on difficult issues, the election of a sympathetic candidate does not eliminate the need for postelection lobbying and monitoring.

SOCIAL WORKERS AND CAMPAIGNS

Innumerable skills carry over easily from social work practice to campaigning, the most obvious being communication skills. Social workers are trained to meet people, listen to their problems, and help them find solutions. They know how to manage hostility, how to reach out to shy and quiet people, and how to deal with groups as well as with individuals (Kleinkauf, 1982). Unfortunately, misinterpretations of the Federal Hatch Act and state-level Hatch acts, fear of agency reprisal, and lack of understanding of how to become involved have kept many social workers from involving themselves in political campaigns. Regardless of the setting in which a social worker is practicing, he or she has numerous useful skills that can be employed in a campaign and, ultimately, through election of sympathetic officials, used to benefit his or her clientele.

The most important skills a social worker can contribute to a campaign are in the area of interpersonal relationships and listening skills. These can be used in many facets of a campaign, for example, in canvassing a neighborhood for support of the candidate, or in working with campaign volunteers and with the candidate.

For most candidates, the entire campaign process is a challenge to their self-confidence, and they must recognize this in order to minimize defensiveness. The social worker's interpersonal skills can be valuable in offering support and reassurance when the candidate is faced with the discouragement that inevitably occurs as the campaign progresses. Just as a candidate needs support, campaign volunteers will need reassurance and motivation, which social workers can provide.

Because social workers must deal daily with a multitude of problems and people, their experience can be particularly valuable to a campaign when positions on issues are being formulated. For example, one candidate was going to take a position, in response to public pressure, that all persons convicted of sexual abuse of children should receive a minimum 10-year prison sentence. Social workers with experience in this problem area pointed out that 70 percent of child sexual abuse occurs in the family, that the abuser usually is the father, that the mother usually is dependent on the abuser and would have to rely on governmental aid if separated from him for the rest of his or her life, that the child involved would carry the guilt of having sent his or her father to jail, and that 10 years of imprisonment would be quite costly to society. The candidate subsequently reversed his stand and instead supported a rehabilitation program designed to deal with the problem.

Because working effectively with individuals and groups is fundamental to social work practice, social workers will find their professional methods more useful in a political campaign than they might have expected (Salcido, 1984).

WHAT TO EXPECT WHEN VOLUNTEERING

A committed and enthusiastic volunteer who meets with voters is second in influence only to the candidate. The effectiveness of such contacts far exceeds the influence of advertising and literature. Thus the wealth of many campaigns is a function of the number of skilled, committed volunteers who are involved.

In some campaigns, nearly every task is performed by volunteers, especially when money is a scarce resource. Some volunteer assignments, in addition to campaign planning, canvassing, and policy making, are listed below.

Clipping newspaper articles	Delivering news releases
Running errands	Monitoring news programs
Putting up signs	Doing research, writing, art work, and the like
Getting out mailings	
Typing	Addressing envelopes
Organizing candidate coffees	Leafleting or letter drops
Making posters	Canvassing (both door-to-door and telephone)
Preparing voter lists	

Mimeographing
Organizing fundraising events
Soliciting contributions
Recruiting additional volunteers
Looking up telephone numbers
Serving as poll watchers

Distributing advertising items at the polls
Babysitting for voters or workers
Serving as messengers
Driving voters to polls

Often social workers who are just beginning campaign work feel frustrated when they are not allowed a great deal of input regarding issues and public concerns but instead are asked to do tasks such as those listed above. They feel that their skills are not being utilized to the fullest, that they would rather use their expertise and skills in managing, consulting, and writing issue papers for the candidate. Indeed, a social worker may have these abilities and the ability to play that role in some campaigns. However, it is usually the campaign manager who has established the solid working relationship with the candidate that is essential to a successful campaign.

The best way for a social worker to be accorded more responsibility in a campaign is to become involved in it very early and to establish a good working relationship with the candidate. Nonetheless, regardless of when a social worker enters the campaign, he or she can make adequate use of other social work skills in conjunction with a variety of campaign tasks, most notably in dealing with people. Tasks may include making telephone calls in response to inquiries or personally contacting constituents. The core of a campaign is interaction with people, and who is better equipped for that than a social worker?

In reality, a campaign is a lot of hard work. It entails many long hours of tedious chores such as those listed above. Many volunteers become dismayed when they work on a campaign because they do so much tedious work, but if the campaign is in tune with the volunteers, they will be shown that what they are doing is an integral part of reaching the campaign's major goal—winning the election.

Social workers understand particularly well the need for balancing volunteer activities, work, and family. However, they must be aware of certain unique characteristics of a campaign in order to survive and be effective. The following are some problems that social workers may encounter within a campaign:

1. The political campaign organization, in contrast to a structured social work agency, is temporary and loosely organized, and, as such, may not be responsive to the psychological and emotional needs of its workers (Salcido, 1984).
2. Conflicts in values and expectations often exist among the diverse groups and numerous individuals involved in the political camapaign. Not all

campaign workers (or even the candidate) may really care about human service issues.

3. Some of the political campaign's administrative and personnel problems, such as stress and uncertainty, are so common that they are considered intrinsic to campaign work and left untouched (Salcido 1984).

4. There is always a lack of time to deal with individual constituent's problems.

5. The many unprofessional activities that must be performed during a campaign, such as licking stamps, can be discouraging to campaign volunteers.

6. Lack of concern within the campaign about issues plus great concern about money can also be discouraging to social work volunteers.

7. The pursuit of one goal, winning the election, leaves both the volunteers and some issues as a secondary concern.

8. Social workers may want the candidate to meet their colleagues, but the candidate, feeling this group is likely to support him or her in any event, may consider such a trip a waste of limited resources that could be used to persuade undecided voters.

One benefit of working on a campaign, in addition to having the candidate's ear, is that the social worker will make a great many contacts in the legal, business, and commercial fields, as well as in other areas of the community. As a result of such contacts, one will often discover shared interests and concerns where none might have been thought to exist. A realtor, for example, may be supporting the social worker's candidate for the same reason as the social worker, namely, lack of adequate housing in the community. Such encounters can prove mutually enlightening. The realtor may gain insight into the need for low-cost housing, while the social worker may learn that an adequate supply of mortgage money at reasonable interest rates is needed for families to buy a home.

HOW TO VOLUNTEER FOR A CAMPAIGN

It might seem ridiculous to include a section on how to volunteer for a campaign, but all too often campaigns start quickly with a core group known to one another, and after a brief period volunteer recruitment largely ceases. Later, the campaign becomes so hectic and confusing that volunteers feel lost and unsupported and drop out.

As previously mentioned, it is best to become involved in a campaign very early. In many instances, a good time to make one's interests known to a prospective candidate is January of an election year. Local party offices generally are quite willing to assist volunteers in connecting with prospective candidates.

The best approach is to make yourself known to the candidate or the campaign manager and ask for an assignment. If one has the skills and the desire to do certain jobs on the campaign, that information should be made known. If your interest is not acknowledged, press again for some form of assignment. It must be remembered that given the lack of time, and the pressures of a campaign, volunteers may fall through the cracks and not be adequately supported or thanked. A person wishing to volunteer often must persist long enough to make it clear that he or she really wants to help. Volunteers should indicate the number of hours and the level of commitment they are willing to give. In return, the volunteer should be given a clear description of what his or her job will entail and any deadlines that must be met.

Even if a social worker feels his or her skills and abilities are not being utilized to the fullest, it is wise not to drop out of the campaign. Because of the pressure and the timing of any campaign, the campaign planning committee must be sure that volunteers are adequately dedicated to the campaign and can be trusted with major responsibilities. Given the highly sensitive nature of a campaign, the short time frame, and the amount of work involved, candidates must be careful to whom responsibility is assigned. If a key task is left undone, it can badly damage chances for achieving the campaign's goal.

Finally, it is important to publicize that social workers are working on a particular campaign. The elected official then will know not only that you assisted in his or her victory, but also, he or she and other legislators as well will know that politically active social workers do exist. Such knowledge may lead the legislator(s) involved to look more favorably upon subsequent lobbying efforts by other members of the social work profession.

CONCLUSION

The campaign is probably the most confusing component of the political process, yet it is at the very heart of it. Participation in a successful political campaign can enhance the effectiveness of subsequent lobbying and monitoring of government agencies and legislation. The campaign offers both excitement and tedious work, and the payoff to the individual social worker and to the profession is much greater than appears on the surface.

Social workers must realize that their skills can be used in various segments of the political arena, but are especially useful during a campaign. There is no greater satisfaction than knowing an elected representative has an understanding of and sympathy for the values exemplified by social work and will respond when a social worker wishes to address, endorse, or recommend a piece of legislation.

ASSIGNMENTS

1. Review different campaign slogans and determine for each what message the candidate is conveying. Surmise from a campaign slogan what positions you think the candidate would have on an issue and then check his or her positions statement to determine if your assumptions are accurate.
2. Volunteer to work on a campaign. After the candidate wins, visit him or her and talk about an issue that concerns you. Determine if your support is received with a willingness to help on the issue now that the campaign is over.
3. Find a person who wants to run for office and work with him or her from the very beginning, to learn every aspect of campaigning. Then compare responses of your candidate with those of the elected official you interviewed for Assignment 2 when you contacted him or her about a issue.

SUGGESTED READINGS

Brager, George A. "Advocacy and Political Behavior." *Social Work*, 13 (April 1968): pp. 5–15.

Kleinkauf, Cecilia. "Running for Office: A Social Worker's Experience." In Maryann Mahaffey and John Hanks (Eds.), *Practical Politics: Social Work and Political Responsibility*. Washington DC: National Association of Social Workers, 1982, pp. 181–194.

Salcido, Ramon M. "Social Work Practice in Political Campaigns." *Social Work*, 29 (March–April 1984): pp. 189–191.

REFERENCES

Campaign Workbook. Washington DC: National Women's Education Fund. 1978.

Kleinkauf, Cecilia. "Running for Office: A Social Worker's Experience." In Maryann Mahaffey and John Hanks (Eds.), *Practical Politics: Social Work and Political Responsibility*. Washington DC: National Association of Social Workers, 1982, pp. 181–194.

Salcido, Ramon M. "Social Work Practice in Political Campaigns." *Social Work*, 29 (March–April 1984): pp. 189–191.

9
Social Workers as Politicians

How often do social workers wonder—after helping a teenage mother find a formula for her three-month-old child or a senior citizen pay for an emergency heating bill, or after informing a client that needed services are unavailable—how many other thousands of people may be facing the same problem?

Social workers assist on a daily basis many clients with diverse problems; although one obvious career choice—to seek political office—would allow a social worker to multiply his or her efforts a hundredfold, few social workers consider a career as a social worker/politician, even though it can have a far-reaching influence on the development and implementation of social policy.

In the Ninety-Eighth Congress, the United States Government spent billions of dollars on human services, but only three social workers were members of the 535-person Congress. In addition, although state appropriations for human services represent a large proportion of state budgets, 40 of the 50 state legislatures had no elected members in 1984 who were social workers.

The purpose of this chapter is to help social workers determine whether to consider the social work/politician career role. It must be remembered, however, many aspects of political life will not be discussed here because they are not necessarily unique to the social worker.

The material for this chapter was obtained from social workers who have held or are now holding public office or who have run for an office in the past. The data was obtained by two methods: interviews and questionnaires. The social workers queried held political offices on boards of education, township councils, county or city commissions, state legislatures, and the United States House of Representatives. All had obtained an MSW and had some social work practice prior to holding political office. Because the National Association of Social Workers does not maintain records on social workers who are employed in political settings, and because of the reluctance of social worker/ politicians to acknowledge their social work background (for political reasons), a snowball sampling approach was necessary to identify respondents.

Questions for the interview and questionnaire were designed to determine what unique difficulties and successes social workers have encountered in the role of politician. The questionnaire consisted of 30 questions, 7 of which gathered demographic data, such as age, sex, marital status, and political affiliation. The remaining questions were open-ended and were intended to elicit information about any successes and problems these respondents experienced as politicians that were related to their social work training. For example, the questions posed included the following: "What event (s) led you to run for office? What, if any, personal stresses or difficulties did you experience either in the campaign or in the office? If you had it to do over again, would you still obtain a degree in social work? If not, in what discipline?

The following findings are presented not only to summarize the information collected from these respondents, but to provide interested social workers with information useful to them in determining their own interest in and aptitude for a political career.

DECIDING TO RUN

Very few individuals who attend a graduate school of social work intend to become a politician, and few, if any, programs exist to teach social workers about politics. As a result, the idea of running for office generally occurs later in a social worker's career and not as a result of graduate specialization.

All of the social worker/politicians who were questioned had been involved in some form of community action or organizing. This is not surprising, since few were clinicians. From these activities they came to realized that their social work background had provided many politically useful skills. Seventy percent indicated they became involved in community organizing because they wanted better solutions to social problems. Eventually these social workers realized that more could be accomplished if they were actually in a political position, thus awakening them to the idea of running for office (Kleinkauf, 1982). Interestingly, all initially discounted the idea of running because they believed that a law degree is necessary for success.

Once awakened to the idea of running for office, many floundered, seeking guidance about how to begin. Because there are no formal means of obtaining such training, social workers who wish to enter the political arena need the benefit of informal support and guidance. When asked where they found this, only the younger politicians indicated mentor support; they also stated that few of these mentors were social worker/politicians. All saw it as advantageous to have assistance from someone who knows the political scene and is supportive of the social worker's efforts.

Ideally, that person would be a social worker/politician, but because such people seldom are available, few of the respondents had social work mentors when running for office; however, many are now political mentors to other social workers.

Several problems are unique to social workers who wish to establish a political career.

1. The agencies in which social workers are employed are often reluctant to support the worker's candidacy for political office, citing "politics" as the reason. Private agencies fear alienating any of their sources of community support. This is particularly true for agencies that rely on community funding. Nor do agency executives want to offend board members who may hold views other than the candidate's on major campaign issues. In state-funded agencies, difficulties arise from state Hatch acts, which often prohibit this type of employee political activity.

2. Agencies usually do not have the flexibility to allow social workers time to campaign. Attorneys in private practice, on the other hand, may be able to reduce workloads during a campaign, unlike social workers, who generally are in full-time staff positions. Social workers in this situation may be forced to take a leave of absence without pay or to resign in order to campaign, and this can create extreme financial difficulties, because social workers usually are paid less than other professionals.

3. The limitation of personal financial resources, already strained by the necessity of a leave of absence, will restrict the amount of money available to finance a first-time campaign. All of the respondents noted that initial campaign funding, particularly for a first campaign, must come from the candidate's own resources.

4. Compared with other professions, the social worker/politician has limited ability to garner campaign support. Attorneys, for example, often can obtain support from their clients, who frequently represent a potentially powerful group of contacts. Social workers, however, cannot ethically use their clients, nor do their clients traditionally have influence or resources likely to assist one in obtaining an office.

Although this list of obstacles is unique to social workers who run for political office, none of our respondents perceived them as monumental. They did, however, emphasize the need to convince a potential social worker/politician that the goal of political office is worth the effort necessary to overcome these obstacles.

Once a social worker decides to run for office, he or she must be doubly able: determined but also able to withstand losing. This was pointed out by all who had lost an election. Every social worker mentioned the need for determination. Many indicated that difficulty arose because of their belief in a life that balances work and family—a value the social work profession also advocates. This problem, which will be discussed later, also occurred while respondents were in office.

BUILDING A CONSTITUENT BASE

Financial support and volunteer efforts are the key elements in a campaign, and later, in success in office. These indispensable resources are particularly important to social worker/politicians. If money is limited, volunteers become even more important to counterbalance this deficit. Although campaign costs varied, volunteer time, skills, and ideological support were of significant importance to all interviewed.

Although the number of supporters is important, the amount of power these constituents have in terms of income, education, or status also is important. That is, to be elected and to remain in office, one must be connected to and representative of a broad spectrum of people. Relating only to selected segments of the population, such as social workers, the poor, or blacks, can easily lead to "labeling" and potential stigmatization. Furthermore, a broad constituent base enhances credibility.

It is well to remember, therefore, that many political issues may fall outside the scope of social work concerns. A social worker/politician must be able to assess ideologies other than those associated with social work. One of the politicians interviewed found himself in the middle of a community conflict between environmentalists and industrial developers over development of a shopping mall. The social work profession obviously does not have a position on such an issue; the social worker/politician formulated his position after assessing his constituent's opinions on this issue.

Given the small numbers in the population who are social workers and the relatively low priority that social workers give to political action, reliance on social workers as a constituent base is unwise, limiting, and potentially harmful to an aspiring social worker/politician. Building bridges to other professions and professional associations, such as lawyers, teachers, and psychologists, is essential for getting elected (Keith-Lucas, 1975).

Social workers may view themselves as being ideologically opposed to many of their constituents—perhaps blue-collar workers, on the one hand, and the upper class on the other. As guardians of the "underdogs," social workers too often have taken a simplistic view of organized labor or the privileged elite as their opponents on social issues. It would be wise to view these groups (and others) as potential collaborators on issues where what is in the best interest of the social work client coincides with the best interest of the general community. Not only is this approach important for getting elected but generally it is the only way a politician can function once elected.

The emergence in the past few years of the "new poor" or the recently unemployed as a major social problem, for example, could well unite organized labor, social workers, and the wealthy to seek solutions that benefit all: that is, solutions that provide incentives to employers to create jobs without reducing wages or increasing taxes. Certainly labor unions and the social work profession have common objectives with respect to this goal.

As mentioned earlier, many of the social workers in our sample had a community organization background. Their grassroots organizing efforts on community issues enabled them to use their experience and personal connections to develop a constituent base. Our respondents included activists in the civil rights movement, bloc associations, human service coalitions, and those in significant positions in the other candidates' campaigns. Such activities provided many with opportunities to establish linkages, gain experience, and build constituent bases.

Building or expanding a constituent base should not be attempted solely on the candidate's position on key issues. In the tradition of "grassroots organizing," soliciting input on individual and community needs and on the relative importance of community problems are excellent methods for identifying and involving potential supporters.

CAMPAIGNING

A central question that immediately confronts the social worker who decides to run for elective office is whether to publicize a social work background or minimize it in the campaign. Although all the social workers sampled included their MSW degree on campaign literature, few highlighted it as part of a campaign strategy.

One United States Congressman, however, effectively used his MSW credentials and social work experience in a race against an attorney, convincing the voters that he had "people" experience whereas his opponent had only "legal" experience. On the other hand, a state representative who chose to emphasize her social work background was unfavorable labeled as a "welfare queen." One's decision is probably influenced by the demographic, political, and ideological characteristics of the total constituency, as well as by the campaign's major issues and the opponent's tactics. For example, if raising AFDC allowances, which would raise taxes, is a volatile issue in a wealthy district, flaunting an MSW may not improve popularity. On the other hand, if legislation is pending to reimburse in-home care of the elderly (Medicaid Waiver), and the district is an aged or aging one, a social work platform may be highly attractive.

The question is not whether the social worker/politician should deny his or her social work identity, but whether the longer-term benefit of election to office warrants emphasizing or minimizing it. As one of the interviewees mentioned, "One should always tell the truth—but not always the entire truth." Related to this dilemma is a second question: Should one always adopt a position consistent with one's social work background, or a position reflecting that of the constituent majority, should it differ from the candidate's own? In a Catholic neighborhood, an avid proabortion stance is unlikely to win votes. This is not to suggest that one's social work training be forgotten, but that the candidate temporarily might need to subjugate it to the immediate goal of gaining office.

In addition to such concerns as one's position on the issues, there is also the matter of campaign skills. The skills most necessary for success, according to the respondents, are varied, and include the following:

1. The "people" skills of listening, responding, persuading, and caring are of primary importance. Historically, these are the core generic skills for social work. Regardless of their area of specialization—community organization or clinical—all social worker/politicians interviewed noted the importance of these skills to politicians and emphasized that they had been acquired during their social work education (Thursz, 1975). If there is something new for the social worker/politician to learn, it is to transfer these skills to nonclients (constituents) and to larger groups.

2. Political skills such as linking, brokering, and advocacy, also part of generic social work training, are invaluable on the campaign trail, where "proof" may be required of the candidate's ability to deliver for his or her constituency. Again, the only skill development needed may be to transfer these skills from case (individual) to class (constituent) brokering and advocacy.

3. Other important political skills include the abilities to consider alternative solutions to problems and to attempt to achieve consensus during a campaign. A demonstrated capacity to seek multiple solutions to a problem may lead voters to view the candidate as flexible, open to compromise, and creative. Achieving consensus requires skills in group process, conflict resolution, and persuasion: All of these characteristics are essential to success in both political life and social work practice. Several social worker/politicians did note one deficit in social work training—the omission of teaching strategies and skills for dealing with confrontation.

4. Negotiation and mediation are prime political skills that are not incompatible with social work practice. Clinicians negotiate daily with clients to arrive at clinical contracts regarding problem assessment, diagnosis, and treatment. Although political negotiations may seem more underhanded and less open than negotiations to establish contracts with clients in treatment, the negotiation and mediation skills utilized are the same and both are necessary for the achievement of mutually agreeable and beneficial ends.

REALITIES OF OFFICE

Like the general public, social workers often hold misconceptions about the benefits and costs of holding political office. Therefore, we asked our respondents about the realities of being an elected representative. These questions covered changes in the office holder's economic and social status after being elected and the effect on family life. Some open-ended questions about the difficulties, problems, and benefits were included.

Holding a political office received mixed reviews from the respondents, all of whom enjoyed their jobs but reported problems as well as benefits. An obvious benefit is the power to influence decisions. One social worker said what he liked most about his job was "power." An elected representative not only has a vote in policy decisions, but has access to the media and can thereby attempt to increase public awareness of social problems.

A social worker/politician can also sensitize other legislators to human needs. For example, one interviewee related a story about transportation tickets that were being provided in large quantities for use by the county's commissioners. The majority of the commissioners wanted to use them as political chips. The social worker on the commission, however, demonstrated that senior citizens were in need of free transportation and convinced the other legislators that use of the tickets by senior citizens would be both a sound social policy and good political practice, because senior citizens are dependable voters.

One difficulty noted by the respondents is the need at times to compromise social work values for political necessity. An example of such a compromise was described by a state representative who had been working unsuccessfully to change the juvenile code. During a past legislative session, a bill had been introduced, with the urging of the Sheriffs' Association, that would have imposed limits on the incarceration of juveniles. The Sheriffs' Association's motive was to reduce costs and overcrowding in the jails. The social worker/politician's motive was to prevent the jailing of juveniles. The social worker/politician supported the bill because the solution, although not ideal, was a great improvement over existing practice.

Two constant problems for all politicians are keeping current on social issues and responding to the continual demands and problems of constituents. An overwhelming majority of respondents indicated that they had little difficulty in these areas, for which they credited their social work training. Many remarked on their success in this area in comparison to that of non-social-worker politicians.

Before running for office, many of the interviewees had believed that a law degree was necessary for political success. Several felt that some courses in law would be helpful, and recommended that schools of social work offer some course work to enable social workers to become more politically active (Jankovic, 1981; Miller, 1980). Only one respondent wished he had pursued law instead of social work, and, parenthetically, that particular respondent had been treated mercilessly during the campaign because he was a social worker.

One of the myths dispelled by the respondents was that economic status is greatly improved after election to office. The reader may be skeptical, as were the authors; however, when the expenses of the campaign and of maintaining an office are deducted, one's net worth seldom increases. The general public may feel that politicians are overpaid, but in reality social work administrators receive salaries comparable to politicians'. Politicians must attend fundraising events in return for support received during the campaign and must join many organizations in order to expand their constituent bases. These additional expenditures often offset any salary increase. Also, social workers, unlike attorneys, cannot anticipate an increase in paying clients after leaving political office. Improving one's short-term or long-term economic status is not likely to be an incentive for a social worker contemplating this career choice.

On the other hand, politics does offer the prospect of high social status, in clear contrast to the relatively low status accorded social workers. Thus, although improved economic status may not be an incentive or reward for the potential social worker/politician, improved social status may be. Seventy-five percent of the respondents reported enhanced social status as a result of contacts and invitations received once they were in office. Despite the public's apparent distrust of politicians, they are, in fact, regarded as community leaders and persons of influence and power.

On the surface, political life appears glamorous and indeed it may be, but in reality, there are many nonglamorous aspects. The respondents confirmed that the job requires hard work and long hours to maintain one's position. The hours invested in political life, particularly during the campaign, strain the social worker/politician's personal life. Public exposure and scrutiny intensifies this strain. Furthermore, the demands to attend social events, glamorous or not, should be met, and constraints on family activities must be accommodated. One respondent noted that her family could not participate in any federally funded project, thus prohibiting her child from using the public swimming pool.

Although these strains are not unique to social worker/politicians, they are particularly relevant to them because of the profession's emphasis on interpersonal relationships. We did not investigate the effect of such stress on family and marital relationships; however, it is evident from the responses of the interviewees that a spouse must be committed to this career choice for it to succeed.

A number of alternatives to holding elected political office also offer an opportunity to define social problems and initiate appropriate solutions. Two of the most common roles that offer such an opportunity are legislative aide and administrative appointee.

RECOMMENDATIONS

We asked our respondents to advise social workers interested in pursuing a political career. Their recommendations to individual social workers included the following:

1. First obtain experience in precinct politics, campaigning for another candidate, lobbying, or any combination thereof.
2. After gaining basic experience and building a constituent base, the potential candidate must be willing to ask for financial and personal support.
3. Candidates cannot be falsely modest about their qualifications and must be comfortable with ideological conflict and confrontation. Compromise and political savvy should be exercised.
4. Social worker/politicians must be cautious about taking exaggerated liberal positions and must be aware that acting in in the best interest of the client or community may require the short-term compromise of social work ideals and values in order to achieve longer-term societal reform.
5. The decision to emphasize or minimize one's social work background must be considered on an individual and constituent basis.

Our respondents also offered some advice concerning social work education and organizations:

1. Social work education should include content on political and legislative processes from an action-oriented perspective—not only a historical, descriptive approach. Content on class advocacy, a highly valued social work ideal, should be reintroduced into all courses.
2. The policy course should include experiential and skill-based assignments and be designed for both graduate- and undergraduate-level students.
3. Social work organizations should become more politically active and aware. They should promote political advocacy as a legitimate professional role. Client data, which may be useful in supporting or opposing legislation, should be obtained.
4. Social work organizations must investigate more closely the legal and regulatory constraints on political activity and organizational members in order to dispel myths about these obstacles.

CONCLUSION

It is clear from our research that social worker/politicians recognize a congruence between political and social work skills. The vast majority of those questioned, whether they came from a clinical or a community organization background, were positive about the appropriateness and logic of social work education and training as a basis for political life. That social workers do not pursue this career choice in greater numbers, therefore, remains a mystery.

Although the pitfalls and difficulties of political office were recognized, almost all of the respondents indicated that they wished to continue in politics and probably would do so. Although social work schools and professional organizations could initiate programs to facilitate this career choice for more social workers, the final choice, of course, rests with the individual.

Despite the respondents' differences in timing, previous experience, and choice of first political activity, the common and recurring recommendation they gave to potential social worker/politicians is that the only absolute prerequisite for success is to get involved. Further, the evidence is conclusive that there is no reason for social workers to expect their entry into politics to be anything but successful.

ASSIGNMENTS

1. Examine the local positions in your community to which officials are elected and determine which would be the most viable one for a social worker to hold. Note the reasons for your choice.
2. Attend a city or county council session to determine whether you would have the expertise to deal with the issues on their agenda. If not, what education, training, or experience would enable you to do so?
3. Work on a candidate's campaign. Analyze the tasks necessary for thorough organization and running of a campaign.

SUGGESTED READINGS

Mathews, Gary. "Social Workers and Political Influence." *Social Service Review*, 56 (December 1982): pp. 616–628.

Ribicoff, Abraham. "Politics and Social Workers." *Social Work*, 7 (April 1962): pp. 3–6.

REFERENCES

Jankovic, Joanne, and Ronald K. Green. "Teaching Legal Principles to Social Workers." *Journal of Education for Social Work*, 17 (Fall 1981): pp. 28–35.

Keith-Lucas, Alan. "An Alliance for Power." *Social Work*, 21 (March 1975): pp. 93–97.

Kleinkauf, Cecelia. "Running for Office: A Social Worker's Experience." In Maryann Mahaffey and John Hanks (Eds.), *Practical Politics*. Washington, DC: National Association of Social Workers, 1982; pp. 181–194.

Miller, Jill. "Teaching Law and Legal Skills to Social Workers." *Journal of Education for Social Work*, 16 (Fall 1980): pp. 87–95.

Thursz, Daniel. "Social Action as a Professional Responsibility and Political Participation." In J. Roland Pennock and John W. Chapman (Eds.), *Participation in Politics*. New York: Lieber-Atherton, 1975, pp. 27–34.

Glossary of Legislative Terms

This glossary of legislative terms defines words and phrases frequently used in the legislative process. It is compiled from a variety of state and federal pamphlets.

ADJOURNMENT SINE DIE   "Adjournment with a day." It marks the end of a legislative session because it does not set a time for reconvening.

ADMINISTRATIVE BILL   A bill proposed or favored by a governor.

ADOPTION   Approval or acceptance; usually applied to amendments or resolutions.

AGENCY BILL   A bill proposed by an executive agency.

AIDE   Legislative staff member, hired or appointed to perform clerical, technical, or official duties.

AMENDMENT   Any alteration made or proposed to be made in a bill, motion, or clause thereof, by adding, changing, substituting, or omitting.

AMENDMENT, CONSTITUTIONAL   Resolution passed by both houses that affects the Constitution; requires approval by voters at a general election. (see Referendum)

APPROPRIATE   To allocate funds.

APPROPRIATION   A legislative authorization of money in a specific amount for a specific purpose. Funds are allotted to the agencies by the budget agency after the appropriation is made by the general assembly.

APPROVED BY GOVERNOR   Signature of a governor on a bill passed by the legislature.

ASSEMBLY   The legislature, made up of a certain number of members; elected from districts apportioned on the basis of population.

AUTHOR   The member who introduces a bill in the house of origin. (see also Sponsor)

BILL   Proposed law presented to the legislature for consideration.

BILL ANALYSIS   Brief summary of the purpose, content, and effect of a proposed measure.

BILL, EMERGENCY   A bill to take effect upon signing by a governor or president.

BILL, PRE-FILED   Bills prepared and filed prior to the opening of a regular session.

BILL ROOM   A room where bills may be studied. Other useful legislative material for reference purposes is also available in the bill room.

BILL, VEHICLE   A bill that is introduced by title only. Because some legislation is complicated to write (for example, a school-aid distribution formula) it may not be ready to file by the filing deadline. The chairperson with responsibility for that measure files the bill under a very broad title to ensure its timely introduction.

BILLS, SPECIAL ORDER OF   An order by the legislative body to consider and reconsider a matter that has been before the legislative body at one time.

BLOC   A group of legislators who have certain interests in common and who may vote together on matters affecting that interest (also called a *caucus*).

BUDGET   An estimate of the receipts and expenditures needed to carry out programs for a fiscal year.

BUDGET AGENCY   An executive agency that prepares the budget document for the governor or the president.

BUDGET BILL   A bill specifying the amounts approved by the general assembly for each program of state government.

BUDGET COMMITTEE   A committee of legislators, which acts in an advisory capacity to the budget agency between sessions of the general assembly (also called *appropriations committee*).

BUDGET, EXECUTIVE   Suggested allocation of state money presented by the governor for consideration by the legislature.

CALENDAR (HOUSE)   A list prepared daily by the Speaker of the bills on second and third readings, which may be acted on that day.

CALENDAR (SENATE)   A daily list of all bills eligible for second or third readings that day.

CHAIR   Presiding officer or chairperson.

CHAMBER   Official hall for the meeting of a legislative body.

CLERK OF THE HOUSE   The chief administrative officer elected by the members.

CODE   A systematic and complete compilation of the laws on a given subject. A code supercedes all prior acts on the subject.

COMMITTEE, AD HOC   Committee appointed for some special purpose. The committee automatically dissolves upon the completion of its specified task.

COMMITTEE CHAIR   A member appointed to function as the parliamentary head of a standing or special committee in the consideration of matters assigned to such committee by the legislative body.

COMMITTEE OF THE WHOLE   A parliamentary device by which the entire membership of one house sits as a committee to consider legislation. Like other committees, it reports back its recommendations to the house.

COMPANION BILL   Two or more bills dealing with related aspects of the same topic (also called *tie bar*).

CONCURRENT RESOLUTION   A statement of the attitude or feeling of the two houses, not having the force of law.

CONCURRENCE   Action by which one house agrees to a proposal or action that the other house has approved. A proposal may be amended, adopted, and then returned to the other house for concurrence.

CONFERENCE COMMITTEE   A bill may be passed by both houses but in differing forms. If the house of origin objects to the version passed by the second house, a special committee is appointed by the leadership of each house to reconcile the differences.

CONSTITUENT   A citizen residing within the district of a legislator.

CONSTITUTIONAL AMENDMENT   A change in the provisions of a constitution by modifying, deleting, or adding portions.

CONSTITUTIONAL MAJORITY A constitutional majority is a bare majority of all members of each house, not merely the majority of members voting on a given issue.

CONTINGENCY FUND Money appropriated by the respective houses for incidental operating expenses.

CONVENE The meeting of the legislature daily, weekly, and at the beginning of a session as provided by the consitution or law.

CONVENTION, CONSTITUTIONAL The assembling of citizens of delegates for the purpose of writing or revising a constitution.

CONVENTION, JOINT The assembling of both houses of the legislature for a meeting.

CO-SPONSOR One of two or more persons proposing any bill or resolution.

DAY CERTAIN Adjournment with a specific day to reconvene.

DEBATE Discussion of a matter according to parliamentary rules.

DIGEST A brief summary of the contents of a bill, which must be attached to the bill before introduction.

DISSENT Difference of opinion; also, to cast a negative vote.

DISTRICT The division of the state represented by a legislator; designated numerically or by geographical boundaries.

DIVISION A method of voting.

DIVISION OF QUESTION Procedure to separate a matter to be voted on into two or more questions.

DO PASS The affirmative recommendation made by a committee in sending a bill to the floor for additional action; *do pass as amended* means a committee recommends certain changes in a bill.

EFFECTIVE DATE A law becomes binding, either on a date specified in the law itself or, in the absence of such date, within a certain number of days specified by constitution or law.

EMERGENCY CLAUSE A phrase added to a bill to make it effective immediately after passage and signing by the governor or president. Laws normally become effective after copies of the acts are distributed to the clerks of the circuit courts.

ENABLING ACT A statute that makes it lawful to do something that otherwise would be illegal. In some states, the legislature enacts a law that becomes operative only on the adoption by the people of an amendment to the constitution.

EN BLOC VOTING To consider in a mass or as a whole. For example: to adopt or reject a series of amendments by a single vote.

ENGROSSING This is a procedure for incorporating any amendments and checking the accuracy of a printed bill.

EX OFFICIO Holding two offices, one of which is held by virtue or because of the first. Example: the lieutenant governor is also a member of the Senate.

EXECUTIVE COMMITTEE ACTION The formal recommendation of a standing committee on any proposal referred to such committee for consideration.

EXECUTIVE SESSION A session excluding from the chamber all persons other than members and essential staff personnel.

FIRST READING To read for the first of three times the bill or title for consideration.

FISCAL NOTE States the estimated amount of increase or decrease in revenue or expenditures and the present and future fiscal implications of pending legislation.

FISCAL YEAR An accounting period of one year.

FLOOR That portion of the assembly chamber reserved for members and officers of the legislature and other persons granted the privilege of the floor.

GALLERY Balconies over chamber from which visitors may view proceedings of the legislature.

GOVERNOR'S PROCLAMATION A means by which the governor may call an extra or special session.

GRANDFATHER CLAUSE Laws providing new or additional professional qualifications often contain a "grandfather clause" exempting persons presently practicing the affected profession from having to comply.

HEARING A session of a legislative committee at which witnesses present testimony on bills under consideration.

HOUSE The federal legislative body more commonly known as the House of Representatives; the lower house of the General Assembly.

HOUSE OF ORIGIN The chamber in which a measure is first introduced is known as its house of origin. A bill is filed either with the Clerk of the House or the Secretary of the Senate, is numbered, and is assigned to a committee. One can determine from a bill's number its house of origin. Numbers given legislation introduced in the House are preceded by HB (House Bill). Numbers assigned Senate bills begin SB (Senate Bill).

IMMEDIATE EFFECT Legislative action to render a law effective at an earlier date than the normal course of events would allow. For example, "Takes effect upon passage" is usually written into the bill.

INTRODUCER One who presents a matter for consideration. Co-introducers are those who subsequently sign a bill or resolution. Primary introducer is the first-named of several introducers.

INTRODUCTION The formal presentation of a bill or resolution for consideration.

JOURNAL An official chronological record of the action taken and proceedings of the respective houses.

LAW Bill passed by both houses and signed by the governor or president allowed to become law without his signature. A bill also may become law if each house, by majority vote, overrides the governor's veto.

LEGISLATIVE STUDY COMMITTEE Frequently an ad hoc committee is established with membership selected by the leadership to work on a controversial subject between sessions, in the hope that legislation acceptable to both houses can be developed.

LOBBYIST A representative of a special interest who attends sessions of the legislature to influence legislation.

MAJORITY LEADER A member of the house chosen by members of the majority party as their leader and floor spokesperson.

MAJORITY PARTY The party having the greater number of members in the legislature of either house.

MAJORITY WHIP A member of the House or Senate designated to perform certain functions, usually of a partisan nature.

MEMBERS ELECT Members who are elected but have not taken the oath of office or are not officially serving.

MEMBERS PRESENT Refers to those members who are actually present at a daily session.

MESSAGE FROM THE SENATE OR HOUSE Official communication from opposite house read into official record.

MINORITY LEADER A member of the minority party designated to be leader.

MINORITY PARTY   Party having the fewest members in the legislature or either house.

MINORITY REPORT   A report that reflects the thinking of the members not favoring the majority position on action on an issue.

MINORITY WHIP   A member of the legislature designated to perform certain functions, usually of a partisan nature.

MINUTES   Accurate record in chronological order of the proceedings of a meeting.

MOTION   Formal proposal offered by a member of a deliberative assembly.

MOTION, MAIN   A consideration of a bill is a main motion. Consideration of an amendment to that bill would be a subsidiary or secondary motion. Consideration of a bill may be postponed. Consideration of an amendment to that bill generally cannot be deferred to another day when the body is to continue its deliberations on the bill, because the body in the meantime may dispose of the main question.

MOTION TO RECONSIDER   A move that places the question in the same status it was in prior to the vote on the question.

NONDEBATABLE   Subjects or motions that cannot be discussed or debated.

OFFICERS   That portion of the legislative staff elected by the membership, (i.e., the speaker of the house, the whip).

OUT OF ORDER   Business that is not conducted under proper parliamentary rules and procedures.

PAIR OR PAIRING   An arrangement between two members of a house by which they agree to be recorded on opposite sides of an issue and to be absent when the vote is taken.

PARLIAMENTARY INQUIRY   Question posed to chair for clarification of a point in proceedings.

PARTY CAUCUS   Each party convenes all its members to elect leaders and establish party positions on specific issues. Party discipline can be very strict, and on certain major issues individual legislators are discouraged from taking independent positions. The party leadership can exert strong influence.

PARTY LEADERSHIP   Within the legislature, party leadership consists of the majority leader (in the House called the Speaker and in the Senate the President Pro Tempore), the minority leader, and their whips. They are elected by their respective caucuses.

PASSAGE OF BILL   Favorable action on a measure before either House.

PER DIEM   Literally, per day; daily expense money rendered legislators and personnel.

PETITION   Formal request submitted by an individual or group of individuals to the legislature.

POINT OF ORDER   Calling attention to a breach of order or rules.

POSTPONE INDEFINITELY   A means of disposing of an issue and by not setting a date to again consider same.

POSTPONE TO A DAY CERTAIN   To deter consideration to a definite later time or day.

PRECEDENT   Interpretation of rulings by presiding officers on specific rules; also unwritten rules that are established by custom.

PREFILE LIST   List of all bills, amendments, and resolutions filed before a session convenes.

PRESIDENT OF THE SENATE   By constitutional enactment the Lieutenant Governor; title of person who presides over the Senate (may vary by state).

PRESIDENT PRO TEMPORE   The majority floor leader in the Senate who presides in the absence of the president of the Senate.

PRESIDING OFFICER   Person designated to preside at a legislative session.

PREVIOUS QUESTION   A motion to close debate and bring the pending question or questions to an immediate vote.

PRINTOUT   Copy of material printed by high-speed computer.

PROCEDURES   Rules and traditional practices of the respective Houses of the legislature.

PROMULGATION   A proclamation of a governor declaring that the acts of the general assembly have been distributed as required by law.

PROOF OF PUBLICATION   A regulation requiring the journal to show that the legislature has determined that notice of intention to apply for passage of any local or special law was published in the affected community the required number of days prior to introduction of the proposed law.

PUBLIC ACTS   Enacted acts.

PUBLIC LAWS   Legislation enacted into law. A bill, as passed both houses of the legislature, that has been enrolled, certified, approved by the governor, or passed over the governor's veto and published.

PUBLICATION CLAUSE   Section incorporated in a bill to enable legislation to become effective on a specific date.

QUESTION, PRIVILEGED   Those questions which, according to rules or by consent of the assembly, shall have precedence.

QUORUM   The number of members of a house who must be present for the body to conduct business.

RATIFY   To approve and make valid.

READING   Presentation of a bill before either house by the reading of the title; a stage in the enactment of a measure.

READING, FIRST   A bill is read aloud on the floor of the House or Senate by title only and is assigned to a committee by the Speaker or the president of the Senate.

READING, SECOND   After a committee finishes its work on a measure, it may report it out of committee. Copies of the legislation are printed and distributed to all members of the appropriate house. At this juncture, called the second reading, debate takes place in the chamber and a bill can be amended, killed, or passed.

READING, THIRD   A bill is reprinted with second-reading changes incorporated. Its title is read for a third time. At this point a two-thirds majority is necessary to amend the bill. A final vote is taken and the legislation either passes or fails.

READY LIST   List of all proposed legislation reported out of committee and ready to be placed on the agenda.

RECALL (A BILL)   Request by a house that the other house or the governor return a bill, usually for a corrective amendment.

RECEDE   Withdraw from an amendment or position on a matter.

RECESS   Intermission in a daily session.

RECOMMIT   To send back to committee for further investigation or to another committee.

RECONSIDERATION   A motion which, when granted, gives rise to another vote annulling or reaffirming an action previously taken.

RECORD   By custom, members of a legislative body often request that the record show a statement or that it be recorded in a certain way; these requests, if approved, are entered in the journal, and are said to be "on the record."

REFERENDUM   A vote at the polls for the purpose of allowing the wishes of the people on a subject to be expressed. A referendum may be held on any issue.

REFERRAL   The sending or referring a bill to committee.

REGULAR ORDER OF BUSINESS   The established sequence of business set up for each legislative day.

REGULATION   A rule or order of an agency promulgated under the authority of a statute passed by the legislature.

REJECTION   An action that defeats a bill, motion, or other matter.

RESCIND   Annulment of an action previously taken.

RE-REFER   The reassignment of a bill or resolution to a committee.

REPEAL   A method by which legislative action is revoked or abrogated.

REPRESENTATIVE   A member of the House of Representatives.

RESOLUTION   A document expressing sentiment or intent of the legislature, governing the business of the legislature, or expressing recognition.

RESOLUTION, JOINT   A form of legislation used to pose amendments. Joint resolutions do not become laws and do not require signature by the governor.

RESOLUTION, SENATE OR HOUSE   Same as concurrent resolution except it is the expression of one house.

REVENUE   Yield of taxes and other sources of income the state collects.

REVISED CODE   Statutory laws of the state.

ROLL CALL   The recording of the presence of members or the taking of a vote on a bill.

ROSTER   Booklet containing names of members, officers, employees, and a list of standing committees and districts of each house for the current session.

RULES   Regulating principles, methods of procedure.

RULES, JOINT   Rules governing the relationship and affecting matters between the two houses.

RULES, STANDING   Permanent rules adopted by each house for the duration of the session.

RULES, SUSPENDED   Temporarily setting aside of rules.

RULES, TEMPORARY   Practices usually adopted at the beginning of each session until standing rules are adopted, generally consisting of the standing rules of the preceding session.

RULES, WAIVE   A procedural step used to forego a rule in order to speed the process of enactment of a measure.

SECOND HOUSE   A house other than the house of origin.

SECRETARY OF THE SENATE   A nonmember officer of the Senate elected or appointed by the members to serve as chief administrative officer.

SECTION   Portion of the codes; sections are cited in each bill that propose to amend, create, or replace same.

SEGMENT   A portion of a bill.

SELECT COMMITTEE   Special committee of legislators, members of the Senate, or member of the House.

SENATE   The upper house of the General Assembly, consisting of 50 members.

SENIORITY   Recognition of prior legislative service, sometimes used in making committee assignments.

SESSION   Period during which the legislature meets.

SESSION, DAILY   Each day's meeting of a legislative body.

SESSION, EXTRAORDINARY   Special session called by and limited to matters specified by the governor.

SESSION, JOINT   Meeting of the two houses together.

SESSION, REGULAR   The annual session at which all classes of legislation may be considered.

SIMPLE RESOLUTION   An expression of the sentiments of one house on matters related to that house. A simple resolution does not require action by the other house.

SINE DIE   Adjournment without a day being set for reconvening. Final adjournment.

SPEAKER OF THE HOUSE   The presiding officer of the House of Representatives, chosen by the members.

SPEAKER PRO TEMPORE   Substitute presiding officer, taking the chair on request of the speaker in his absence; elected by the body.

SPECIAL ORDER   Matter of business set for a special time and day designated.

SPONSOR   A member who agrees to introduce and support a bill in the second house after its passage by the house of origin. (*See also* Author).

STANDING COMMITTEE   Regular committees of the legislature set up to perform certain legislative functions.

STATE THE QUESTION   To place a question before a legislative body for its consideration.

STATUTORY COMMITTEE   A committee created by statute.

STOPPING THE CLOCK   Practice of lengthening the hours of the legislative day, irrespective of the passing of the hours of the calendar day.

STRIKE OUT   Delete language from a bill or resolution.

STRIPPING   The entire contents of one bill may be deleted and a completely new measure inserted under the title of the old bill. It is a technique employed to resurrect a measure that may have died in committee.

SUBSTITUTE   An amendment that replaces an entire bill or resolution.

SUFFICIENT SECONDS   The support of the number of members required to make certain motions and procedures.

SUPPLEMENTAL APPROPRIATION   Adjustment of funds allocated over the original allocation.

TABLE   A means of disposing of a bill or other matter for an indefinite period of time.

TERM   Duration of office of an elected official.

TITLE   Statement of the general subject of a bill.

UNANIMOUS CONSENT   Usually requested to suspend rules for a specific purpose.

UNFINISHED BUSINESS   Business that has been laid over from a previous day.

UNIFORM AND MODEL ACTS   Legislation recommended by various national groups for passage in all or several states. Uniform acts are prepared by the Conference of Commissioners on Uniform State Laws and are intended to be adopted verbatim by the various states. Model acts are prepared by numerous organizations to serve as guides for state legislation and may be modified to suit each individual state.

VETO   The president's or governor's disapproval of a bill passed by both houses of the general assembly. The governor is allowed a set number of days to sign or veto a bill or allow it to become law without his signature. Bills vetoed during a session must be returned to the house of origin for reconsideration and vetoes may be overridden by the vote of a constitutional majority in each house.

VETO OVERRIDE   To pass a bill over the president's or governors' veto.

VOICE VOTE   Oral expression of the members when a question is submitted for their determination. Response is given by *ayes* and *nays* and the presiding officer states the decision as to which side prevailed.

VOTE, DIVISION AND RISING   To vote by a show of hands or by standing.

VOTE, EN BLOC   To dispose of several items, such as a series of amendments, by taking one vote.

VOTE, RECORD   A roll call vote in which each member answers to his or her name and announces that he or she is voting yea or nay. The vote is recorded in the journal.

VOTE, ROLL CALL   Individual votes of members are recorded in the journal.

VOTE   Formal expression of will or decision by the body.

WHIP   An elected member whose duty is to keep the rest of the members informed as to the decisions of the leadership.

WITHDRAW A MOTION   To recall or remove a motion according to parliamentary procedure.

WITHOUT RECOMMENDATION   A committee report that is neither favorable or unfavorable.

YEAS AND NAYS   Recorded vote of members on an issue.

YIELD   The relinquishing of the floor to another member to speak or ask a question.

Index